A Handbook of Pet Care and Management

A Handbook of
Pet Care and Management

DR. AMITA RANJAN
Department of Veterinary Pharmacology & Toxicology
College of Veterinary Sciences
Guru Angad Dev Veterinary and Animal Sciences University
Ludhiana-141 004, Punjab

SSPH

SATISH SERIAL PUBLISHING HOUSE
403, Express Tower, Commercial Complex
Azadpur, Delhi-110033 (India)
Phone : 011-47073040, Fax : 91-11-27672046
e-mail : info@satishserial.com, hkjain1975@yahoo.com
Website : www.satishserial.com

Published by :

SATISH SERIAL PUBLISHING HOUSE
403, Express Tower, Commercial Complex, Azadpur, Delhi-110033 (INDIA)
Phone : 011-47073040, Fax : 91-11-27672046
E-mail : info@satishserial.com, hkjain1975@yahoo.com

Print Again, 2023

ISBN : 978-93-81226-07-0

Composed, Designed & Printed in India

Preface

It is my great pleasure to bring out this small book on care and management of pet dogs. I have tried to describe all the essential aspects related to dog keeping in a concise manner, aiming to answer queries of novice pet owners, dog breeders and undergraduate veterinary students. Few topics covered in this book are least reviewed by other authors. I hope, readers will enjoy reading this book and find it informative as well.

No book can be claimed to be perfect and complete in all aspects. Scope of improvement is always left. I sincerely look forward towards readers for critical suggestions.

It is my privilege to thank Dr. Rakesh Ranjan, my husband for his valuable suggestions and constant encouragements. I express gratitude to my colleagues, teachers, field veterinarians for their valuable support.

I am thankful to Hemant Jain, Satish Serial Publishing House for publishing the book in a nice form.

At the last, I express regards, gratitude and thank to my father-in-law, the first reader of this book, for corrections and valuable inputs. I also express thanks to family members and friends, as without their whole heartedly support, it would have been impossible to complete this manuscript.

Amita Ranjan

Contents

Chapter 1

Keeping Dogs as Pet

Why to keep a dog?

Since times immemorial, dogs have been kept as pet. They provide loyal companionship, can fulfill emotional gaps and alleviate sufferings of people in distress, depression, loneliness and anxiety. Dog keeping is beneficial, particularly for persons with hypertension, epilepsy and mental retardation. Dogs may be trained to work with and help people with physical disabilities. Dog keeping provokes social interaction, inculcates sincerity and keep away your children from watching television or playing video-games all the leisure time. Moreover, in a nuclear family where both husband and wife are working, the dogs provide a good alternative guard to your lonely home. But in such case, it is advised to give a company to the dog by rearing another dog of opposite sex or cat. Dogs are also kept sometimes for sport, hunting and working. There are some astrological points and myths also. It is a common belief that keeping a black dog in the house protects the family from ill effects of "Shani" grah. A black dog also nullifies all the negative energy. If you have a naughty and destructive child, keeping a black dog may be helpful.

This is one side of the picture. There are some undesirable/ harmful effects also. Dogs can transmit a variety of infections, specially to children. It does not mean that one should not rear pets. If you have a dog, always maintain good hygiene and adopt certain precautionary measures to minimize chances of disease transmission. Remember, 'only a healthy dog can provide a healthy companionship'.

When to start dog keeping?

The ideal time to bring a new pup/dog in your family is when your child is at least five years old. At this age, he will be physically strong enough not only to give a good company, but also to control its mischievous behavior, if any. Besides, a young child due to over enthusiasm and mishandling, may harm the small pup. On the other hand, a strong stout pup or dog may knock the child. It is not advisable to bring a pup in one's family when a child is expected. A pup or a dog may feel jealous while observing that more attention is given to a newcomer (baby) instead of him. If you have to visit abroad or stay outstation for long time in coming years, or your job demands frequent outstation visits, bringing a dog home is not advisable. Dog can serve a good companion for older people, when their children have left home, but again their physical capabilities are to be taken into consideration.

How to select a dog?

Several points should be considered before selecting a dog. Availability of space, family members, their leisure hours, age group and love for dogs should always be considered first. The adult size, nature, personality, food and exercise requirement varies with dog breed. German Shepherd, Poodle, Australian Sheepdog, Labrador Retriever are intelligent dogs. Pug, Cocker Spaniel, Beagle, Labrador Retriever and Golden Retriever are friendly with children. Pug, Bulldog, Lhasa Apso, Dachshund, Basenji, Boston Terrier, German Spitz, Pomeranian, Chihuahua and Pekingese are good options for cities, where limited space is available. They do not require much exercise. German Shepherds, Rotweiller, Saint Bernard, Napolian Mastiff, Boxer, Dalmatian and Doberman are good guard dogs. Grey hounds, Afghan Hound, and Rampur Hound are good for sports.

Pup or Adult?

The decision to bring a new pup or an old dog should be taken on the basis of your need and family circumstances. A pup is playful and adorable, and develops strong relationship with the owner. If young members are there in the family, bringing a pup is advisable. However, a pup needs a lot of time and care specially during first few weeks. One person should be always available for care, feeding and toilet training. Pups like our children, are more susceptible to cold exposure and various infectious diseases. Any negligence to its housing, feeding or vaccination can result in serious health troubles that may take several days to cure. A sick pup often becomes a problem if all members of the family are old or working.

If you are looking for a good companion or searching a guard, go for bringing an adult dog. For elder people, an adult dog will be easier to keep and manage. However, one will have to be patient and work overtime to establish a strong relationship with the dog. Initially the dog may be nervous or aggressive in the new house with new owners. Some breeds may even be dangerous if there is a small baby in the house.

Male or Female?

Both male and female have pros and cons. Female is easy to handle and train, more friendly with children and generally does not like frequent outdoor visits. However, they come in heat (breeding cycle) twice a year, which is accompanied by bloody vaginal discharges and gathering of male dogs from the neighborhood. They are prone to develop infected wombs (uterus) and mammary gland tumors. These problems, however, can be prevented by surgical de-sexing.

Male dogs are often dominating in nature, and therefore, hard to handle and train. They enjoy roaming outside and may become restless during breeding period, especially if any bitch in heat is present in the nearby area. But males are better as watchdogs and intruder deterrents and demand less attention and care.

Small or Large Breed?

Depending upon the body size of the adult dog, different breeds can be divided into two groups, small breeds and large breeds. Large breed dogs are good as watch dog, but expensive, both to buy and feed. They require more exercise and hence more manpower for management. They are not suitable for metropolitan cities or small houses or flats, and where family members are either old or busy in work.

Small breeds are less costly to buy and maintain. They need less exercise; virtually they exercise themselves in the house or garden. They are easy to handle and more friendly with children. They can also alarm and deter intruders by barking. They are rather the best for middle class families.

Long or Short Hair-coat?

While selecting a breed, consideration should also be given to their hair coat. Dogs with long hair coat, like German Shepherd, Cocker Spaniel, Golden Retriever, St Bernard, Labrador, Bhutia etc. are more prone to develop skin diseases. Besides, they shed old hair coat twice a year and fallen hairs may create a nuisance in the house, particularly if any member of the family is allergic or asthmatic. This problem is less encountered in dogs with short hair coat like Dash Hound, Pug, Doberman, Dalmatian *etc.*

Purebred/ Crossbred or Mongrel?

Decision to purchase a purebred (pedigree) or crossbred or mongrel dog depends mainly on two factors, the first is the amount of money you want to invest and the second is the purpose of dog-keeping. If one wants to keep the dog for breeding purpose or as a status symbol or participation in dog shows, a registered purebred dog is better. One can guess well about their adult size, temperament, feeding and exercise requirements. But, they are more prone to various diseases and congenital abnormalities. Crossbred dogs are hardy, less susceptible to diseases and require less care and attention. They are good, if kept for company or as intruder deterrent. For those who want minimum investment in terms of money, time and labour, a mongrel dog is the best option. They are active, clever, disease resistant, less costly to feed and easy to maintain.

Choosing a pup

Before choosing a pup from a litter (pup mates), examine thoroughly and test the following points:

1. Watch all puppies of the bitch while playing. The full grown, good looking, active pup should be selected. Pup should be neither too shy, nor too bold.
2. Test for hearing and vision. The alert pup which responds to your activity is good. A pup not responding any stimuli, like clapping, loud sounds etc. should be declared unfit.

3. Examine the eyes; it should be shining and free from discharges or opacities or eyelid abnormality.
4. Ears should be clean and free from off smell, discharges or ticks.
5. Make sure that there is no abnormality in jaws. Teeth should be in one line. When mouth shuts, teeth should clamp down on the top of each other.
6. Examine for any lump present around the naval region. It may be hernia. Do not select such pup.
7. Pups should pass well-formed faeces and should be free from signs of diarrhea (Look for wet or soiled tail of the pup).
8. Pup should not be pot bellied. Examine it with fingers for muscle mass and tone. A lean and thin pup with long hairs may look healthy.
9. If you are purchasing a male dog for breeding purposes, examine testicles. Both the testicles should be present in the scrotum of a dog older than 6 months. In a pup less than 6 months old, testicles may or may not be present, since they may not descend from abdomen at this stage.
10. Examine different body parts for any abnormality, particularly for congenital defects, like cleft palate, absence of anal opening (atresia ani) etc. Consult a veterinarian, if any doubt arises.

❑❑❑

Chapter 2

Dog Breeds

More than 850 dog breeds exist across the globe. Many of them are non-descript or local breeds, not recognized by International Kennel Clubs. There are 161 dog breeds recognized by American Kennel Club, while more than 175 breeds are recognized by The Kennel Club, UK. Almost all the dog breeds, except toys, were developed for some specific purpose/ work.

Classification

American Kennel Club classify all pedigree dog breeds into eight groups, i.e. Sporting; Hound; Working; Terrier; Toy; Non-sporting; Herding and Miscellaneous group. The U.K. Kennel Club classification includes seven groups, i.e. Hound; Gundog; Terrier; Utility; Working; Pastoral and Toy group. The British system of classification seems to be more rational and more acceptable worldwide including India.

Hound Group

Breeds originally used for hunting either by scent or by sight. The scent hounds include the Beagle and Bloodhound and the sight hounds include Whippet and Greyhound. They are, in general, dignified and aloof but trustworthy animals that require plenty of exercise, space and training since early days. Some are small sized and can serve as a good family dog. Following breeds come under this group:

Afghan Hound, Azawakh, Basenji, Basset Bleu, De Gascogne, Basset Fauve De Bretagne, Basset Griffon Vendeen (Grand; Petit), Basset Hound, Bavarian Mountain Hound, Beagle, Bloodhound, Borzoi, Cirneco dell'Etna, Dachshund (Long Haired; Miniature Long Haired; Smooth Haired; Miniature Smooth Haired; Wire Haired; Miniature Wire Haired), Deerhound, Finnish Spitz, Foxhound, Grand Bleu De Gascogne, Greyhound, Hamiltonstovare, Ibizan Hound, Irish Wolfhound, Norwegian Elkhound, Otterhound, Pharaoh Hound, Portuguese Podengo (Warren Hound), Rhodesian Ridgeback, Saluki, Segugio Italiano, Sloughi and Whippet.

Gun dogs

Gun dogs were developed to find out the live game (animals) and/or to retrieve the shot and wounded game. This group is divided into four categories - Retriever, Spaniels, Pointer and Setter. They are very intelligent dogs that can be easily trained. In general, they are good family dogs, behave well with children, but not very effective for guarding purposes. Require a lot of exercise. Following breeds come under this group:

Bracco Italiano, Brittany, English Setter, German Longhaired Pointer, German Pointer (Shorthaired, Wirehaired), Gordon Setter, Hungarian Vizsla (Normal, wirehaired), Irish Setter (Normal, Red and White), Italian Spinone, Kooikerhondje, Korthals Griffon, Lagotto Romagnolo, Large Munsterlander, Pointer Retriever (Chesapeake Bay), Retriever (Curly Coated, Flat Coated, Golden, Labrador, Nova Scotia Duck Tolling), Slovakian Rough Haired Pointer, Small Munsterlander, Spaniel (American Cocker, American Water), Spaniel (Clumber, Cocker, English Springer, Field, Irish Water, Sussex,Welsh Springer), Spanish Water Dog and Weimaraner.

Terrier group

Most of the terrier breeds originated in the British Islets and mainly developed for hunting vermin (Latin word "Terra" means earth). They are compact and brave animals with beautiful hairs. Typical terrier temperament is alert, quick and sometimes fiery. Following breeds come under this group:

Airedale Terrier, Australian Terrier, Bedlington Terrier, Border Terrier, Bull Terrier (Standard, Miniature), Cairn Terrier, Cesky Terrier, Dandie Dinmont Terrier, Fox Terrier (Smooth, Wire), Glen of Imaal Terrier, Irish Terrier, Kerry Blue Terrier, Lakeland Terrier, Manchester Terrier, Norfolk Terrier, Norwich Terrier, Parson Russell Terrier, Scottish Terrier, Sealyham Terrier, Skye Terrier, Soft Coated Wheaten Terrier, Staffordshire Bull Terrier, Welsh Terrier and West Highland White Terrier.

Utility groups

This is a diverse group that contains dogs of different shapes and sizes which do not fit under any other group. Most of them were bred to perform specific functions (utility) other than sporting or working. In general, they are good companion dogs. Following breeds come under this group:

Akita, Boston Terrier, Bulldog, Canaan Dog, Chow Chow, Dalmatian, Eurasier, French Bulldog, German Spitz (Klein, Mittel), Japanese Akita Inu, Japanese Shiba Inu, Japanese Spitz, Keeshond, Korean Jindo, Lhasa Apso, Mexican Hairless (Standard, Intermediate, Miniature), Poodle (Standard, Miniature, Toy), Schipperke, Schnauzer, Shar Pei, Shih Tzu, Tibetan Spaniel and Tibetan Terrier.

Working group

This group includes all the non-sporting varieties. They have been developed to provide services like fighting, guarding, guiding the blind, searching explosives and drugs etc. They require regular exercise; otherwise become destructive. They are, in general good family dogs, but some require obedience training to behave properly. Following breeds come under this group:

Alaskan Malamute, Beauceron, Bernese Mountain Dog, Bouvier Des Flandres, Boxer, Bullmastiff, Canadian Eskimo Dog, Dobermann, Dogue De Bordeaux, Entlebucher Mountain Dog, German Pinscher, Giant Schnauzer, Great Dane, Greater Swiss Mountain Dog, Greenland Dog, Hovawart, Leonberger, Mastiff, Neapolitan Mastiff, Newfoundland, Portuguese Water Dog, Pyrenean, Rottweiler, Russian Black Terrier, St. Bernard, Siberian Husky and Tibetan Mastiff.

Pastoral group

Breeds of this group were developed for working in pasture with cattle, sheep and reindeer herds. They have a waterproof double coat to protect from rain and other adverse climatic conditions. Following breeds come under this group:

Anatolian Shepherd Dog, Australian Cattle Dog, Australian Shepherd, Bearded Collie, Belgian Shepherd Dog, (Groenendael, Laekenois, Malinois, Tervueren), Bergamasco, Border Collie, Briard, Catalan Sheepdog, Collie (Rough, Smooth), Estrela Mountain Dog, Finnish Lapphund, German Shepherd Dog (Alsatian), Hungarian Kuvasz, Hungarian Puli, Komondor, Lancashire Heeler, Maremma Sheepdog, Norwegian Buhund, Old English Sheepdog, Polish Lowland Sheepdog, Pyrenean Mountain Dog, Pyrenean Sheepdog (Long Haired), Samoyed, Shetland Sheepdog, Swedish Lapphund, Swedish Vallhund and Welsh Corgi (Cardigan, Pembroke).

Toy Group

This is a diverse group of small dogs developed as companion or lap dog. They require less space and little exercise, are easy to maintain and ideal companion in metros. Following breeds come under this group:

Affenpinscher, Australian Silky Terrier, Bichon Frise, Bolognese, Cavalier King Charles Spaniel, Chihuahua (Long Coat, Smooth Coat), Chinese Crested, Coton De Tulear, English Toy Terrier (Black and Tan), Griffon Bruxellois, Havanese, Italian Greyhound, Japanese Chin, King Charles Spaniel, Lowchen (Little Lion Dog), Maltese, Miniature Pinscher, Papillon, Pekingese, Pomeranian, Pug and Yorkshire Terrier.

Table 1 : Important dog breeds and their character

Labrador Retriever
Gentle, family-oriented, adaptable, and friendly dogs, willing to learn and easy to train. Some may be aggressive or shy. Require lots of exercise, space and human companionship. Poor guarding potential. Colour: Yellow, Black and Chocolate Adult height, weight and life expectancy: 50-60 cm, 27-32 Kg, 12-14 years Hair coat and grooming requirement: Short and dense coat; little grooming required Caution: Prone for obesity.
Golden Retriever
Reliable, friendly and affection-demanding ideal family dog, requires lots of exercise and space. Behave nicely with children. Often used as guide-dog for blind. Poor guarding potential.

Colour: Cream, wheat, light to dark gold

Adult height, weight and life expectancy: 50-60 cm, 25-30 Kg, 13-14 years

Hair coat and grooming requirement: Flat or wavy hairs; regular grooming required

---

Pointer

Very energetic, gentle, intelligent, obedient and hardy dogs, easy to train. But some may be timid. Good with children. Poor guarding potential.

Colour: White background with patches of black, lemon or orange coloured or tricoloured

Adult height, weight and life expectancy: 60-65 cm, 25-34 Kg, 13-14 years

Hair coat and grooming requirement: Short, smooth, dense, glossy and fine hairs; little grooming is required

---

Cocker Spaniel

Affectionate, active and adaptable dog, good with children and easy to train. May bark a lot or turn destructive in boredom. Regular ear cleaning is required. Mostly long lived. Fair guarding potential.

Colour: Vivid colour combinations; mostly white background with big black/ brown patches

Adult height, weight and life expectancy: 35-40 cm, 13-16 Kg, 13-14 years

Hair coat and grooming requirement: Long, silky, slightly wavy hairs with dense protective undercoat, lots of grooming is required

Caution: Prone for progressive retinal atrophy, obesity, behavioral problems, skin and kidney diseases.

Bull Terrier

Types: Standard, miniature, colored and solid white

Mostly intelligent, courageous, enthusiastic but easy to train, strong, active, energetic and hardy. Behaves well with children. If not stimulated, feels boredom. Some dogs may be nervous, difficult to train, fight till death with other animals.

Colour: White or white with coloured (black/ red/ fawn) marking on head and body

Adult height, weight and life expectancy: 50-55 cm, 24-31 Kg (11-15 Kg-Miniature), 11-13 years

Hair coat and grooming requirement: Short, fine, harsh and glossy coat; require little grooming

Caution: Genetically susceptible to deafness, kidney failure, heart and skin diseases

Pekingese

Chinese breed ('Peke' means 'Little Lion Dog'). Independent, aloof, self-confident, courageous but affectionate. Intelligent dog, likes to be the center of attention.

Colour: Red, fawn, black, tan, white and albino

Adult height, weight and life expectancy: 15-20 cm, 2-8 Kg, 12-13 years

Hair coat and grooming requirement: long, straight, profuse hairs, outer-coat coarse; frequent combing is required to prevent matting of hairs.

Caution: Susceptible to eye and respiratory/ breathing problems. Heat stroke is common due to long hairs.

Doberman Pinscher

Fearless, energetic and watchful dog of German origin. Needs proper training to overcome natural wildness. Ears and tail are cropped for show. Require little exercise. Very good guarding potential. Behaves well with own family.

Colour: Black, brown, fawn with red-rust markings on head, chest and feet

Adult height, weight and life expectancy: 65-70 cm, 30-40 Kg, 12 years

Hair coat and grooming requirement: Short, thick, smooth/hard; little grooming is required

Caution: Prone to heart diseases, not good with other pets and strangers, some may be aggressive or nervous

---

Great Dane

Very large and tall with clean appearance. Developed in Germany by crossing Mastiff and Greyhound. Gentle, affectionate but courageous. Needs companionship. Becomes destructive in boredom. Behave well with own family and easy to train. Very good guarding potential. Short lived, needs lots of food and space.

Colour: Black, fawn, light gray with black strips

Adult height, weight and life expectancy: 75-80 cm, 45-55 Kg, 10 years

Hair coat and grooming requirement: Short, thick, glossy, smooth; little grooming required

Caution: Susceptible to arthritis and other bone problems. Some may be timid or aggressive and uncontrollable, if not properly trained

---

Saint Bernard

Swiss dog with large and muscular body. Affectionate, docile, loves children, intelligent and easy to train. Needs lots of space, food and regular exercise. Drools saliva during summer. Good guarding potential

Colour: Red/ brown/ yellow/ orange with white on muzzle, on the top of head, face, chest, forelegs, feet and tail

Adult height, weight and life expectancy: 65-75 cm, 50-90 Kg; 11 years

Hair coat and grooming requirement: Short hairs with thick and dense coat, medium to long length, straight to wavy hairs. Regular grooming is required.

Caution: Susceptible to hip dislocation. Hair shedding is a common problem.

Rottweiler

Strong, muscular, robust, fearless, hardworking and very intelligent dog of German origin (named after City Rottweil). Very good as a guard dog, watchdog or police dog. May be aggressive towards other dogs and strangers. Only properly trained and socialized dog behaves well with children. Requires plenty exercise daily.

Colour: black with rust, rich tan, or brown markings on muzzle, chest, feet, eyes and beneath tail

Adult height, weight and life expectancy: 60-68 cm, 42-50 Kg, 11-12 years

Hair coat and grooming requirement: Double coated, outer coat is of medium length, flat, coarse and dense; undercoat is fine. Little grooming is required.

Caution: Becomes aggressive if not properly socialized and trained or kept chained. Some may be shy, nervous or aggressive by nature.

German Shepherd/ Alsatian

Types: long and short haired

Very intelligent, obedient, fearless and courageous dog that requires regular exercise, proper training and socialization. Erect ears, long hairy tail. Very good family dog, but requires lot of space and food. Excellent as guard, police and guide dog.

Colour: black, tan, cream

Adult height, weight and life expectancy: 60-70 cm, 38-40 Kg, 12-13 years

Hair coat and grooming requirement: Water proof, double coated, inner coat-medium: dense, thick, stiff, flat and coarse; outer coat-long: luxurious

Caution: Some dogs may be nervous, aggressive and vicious particularly if not trained properly. Susceptible to arthritis, hip displacement, eye diseases, gastric and skin problems.

Dachshund

Types: on size basis: standard and miniature; on hair coat basis: short- hair, wire- hair, long/smooth-hair

Alert, active, intelligent, self-willed, brave and dominant dog of German origin. Short-hair breed appear clean with low hair shedding and doggy smell.

Colour: Variable

Adult height, weight and life expectancy: Standard: 20-25 cm, 7-15 Kg, Miniature: 12-20 cm, Below 5 Kg; 14-17 years

Hair coat and grooming requirement: short/ wire/ long; grooming requirement is variable

Caution: Susceptible to back problems, obesity and false pregnancy. May be aggressive with other pets, children and strangers.

Bulldog

Strong, muscular, gentle, courageous dog originated from Great Britain. Pushed-in-snout, fat face and wrinkled loose skin on face. Intelligent dog, easy to train. Requires little exercise. Head shape is the most important feature for judging in dog show.

Colour: Shades of red brindle, solid white, red or fawn, fallow or piebald (variable and not important for judging in dog show).

Adult height, weight and life expectancy: 35-40 cm, 18-25 Kg; 9-11 years

Hair coat and grooming requirement: Fine/ short and straight; little grooming is required.

Caution: Susceptible to skin diseases (skin fold pyoderma), allergies and respiratory problems (due to short snout)

Boxer

Playful, boisterous, brave and intelligent dogs that may remain puppyish throughout the life. Needs proper training from early life. Requires moderate exercise. Very good guarding potential, behaves nicely with children.

Colour: Fawn (light yellow to dark red), brindle with white markings on muzzle, neck, chest and feet

Adult height, weight and life expectancy: 45-60 cm, 23-34 Kg; 12 years

Hair coat and grooming requirement: Short, shiny, close lying and smooth; little grooming is required

Caution: Susceptible to heart diseases, bone, joint and skin problems. Protect from excessive cold and hot weather. Some may be aggressive or shy; not good for strangers.

Chinese Shar-Pei

Intelligent, brave and dominant dog with hippopotamus shaped snout and loose wrinkled skin on head and neck. Ears small; tongue blue black; sand-textured skin; bristly/prickly skin

Colour: Sable, albino, brindle and spotted

Adult height, weight and life expectancy: 45-50 cm, 18-25 Kg, 11-12 years

Hair coat and grooming requirement: Sand-textured skin, horse-coated (short and stiff), brush-coated (slightly longer hairs), and bear-coated (long, soft and cottony hairs) varieties; regular brushing and skin care is required

Caution: Susceptible to many genetic/ inherited eyelids, skin and kidney diseases. Can be aggressive towards other dogs. Protect from heat.

Pug

One of the oldest dog breeds developed in China from Mastiff. Muscular compact body with flat- face, rose or button nose and coiled tail (pig tail). Happy, intelligent, loving, playful, energetic, pugnacious and strong-willed dog, ideal for companionship or as watchdog for people living in cities. Easy to manage and very good with children. Requires little space and exercise.

Colour: Fawn, silver, apricot-fawn with black background

Adult height, weight and life expectancy: 25-33 cm; 6-10 Kg; 13-15 years

Hair coat and grooming requirement: Fine, short, soft, glossy; little grooming required.

Caution: Requires patience to train. Susceptible for obesity, joint, bone, eye, heart and respiratory problems. Protect from extremes of climatic conditions. Tends to snore (noise produced during breathing). Overexertion may cause breathing problems.

Dalmatian

Long lived, lively, intelligent, friendly dog developed in Croatia. Good for guarding purposes and children. Easy to maintain, ideal for companionship in city life. Clean and odorless body, but frequent hair shedding may be a problem.

Colour: White with liver or black spots (evenly distributed spots fetches good marks in dog shows)

Adult height, weight and life expectancy: 48-60 cm, 22-25Kg, 12-14 years

Hair coat and grooming requirement: Short, dense, smooth and glossy; moderate grooming requirement.

Caution: Sheds coat. Susceptible for deafness and urinary problems. May be aggressive towards other dogs.

Lhasa Apso

Intelligent, attractive, amusing, and calm dog originated in China. Ideal for companionship and watchdog. Requires moderate exercise but lot of care for hair coat maintenance. Barks a lot, but behaves very well with children.

Colour: Variable

Adult height, weight and life expectancy: 25-28 cm, 6-9 Kg, 13-14 years

Hair coat and grooming requirement: Top-coat-very long, straight, hard and dense; under-coat-medium length and soft; regular grooming is essential.

Caution: Protect from hot weather. May be hyper-reactive to sound and strangers. Protect eyes from long hairs, trim if required.

Chow Chow

Types: Rough and smooth

Sturdy, muscular, intelligent, stubborn dog originated from Sptiz in China. Peripheral vision is limited, so always approach the dog from front. Good for hunting and guard purposes. Do not behave well with other pets and children.

Colour: Red, black, blue, cream/white, fawn

Adult height, weight and life expectancy: 40-55 cm; 20-32 Kg; 11-12 years

Hair coat and grooming requirement: Under-coat- dense and rough and guard-hairs; Daily grooming is essential

Caution: Some may be aggressive or shy.

Samoyed

Beautiful, intelligent, obedient and active dog used for hunting by Samoyed people of Siberia. Very good with children. Barks a lot; affectionate, adaptable and easy to manage.

Colour: White, cream, biscuit or a combination thereof

Adult height, weight and life expectancy: 40-50 cm, 15-27 Kg, 10-13 years

Hair coat and grooming requirement: Inner-coat: thick, soft and small; outer-coat: long, harsh and glossy

Caution: Sheds a lot of hairs

Greyhound

One of the oldest dog breeds originated in Egypt. Long, lean and arched body with long sharp-pointed muzzle. High running speed and extraordinary stamina and endurance. Mostly noble and gentle in nature, affectionate to family. Racing dog and hence requires a lot of exercise. Good guarding potential. Behaviour with children is variable.

Colour: Black, fawn, white or any other colour

Adult height, weight and life expectancy: 70-75 cm; 25-32 Kg; 11-13 years

Hair coat and grooming requirement: Fine, short and smooth; little grooming is required

Caution: Some may be aggressive. Needs firm control.

Beagle

Intelligent, happy and loyal dog originated in England. Good for guarding purposes. Loves other pets and children.

Colour: Usually tricoloured

Adult height, weight and life expectancy: 32-38 cm, 12-18 Kg, 11-13 years

Hair coat and grooming requirement: Short; little grooming is required

Caution: Susceptible for obesity. May roam aimless.

Afghan Hound

Beautiful, loyal dog with variable temperament. Requires a lot of exercise. Not good for children and strangers.

Colour: Cream, gray, black, black and rust

Adult height, weight and life expectancy: 67-70 cm, 23-25 Kg, 11-12 years

Hair coat and grooming requirement: Long, silky and fine; regular brushing is required.

Caution: Proper training is essential for good behaviour.

Pomeranian

Small dog with compact body, developed in Pomerania (Poland) from white spitz of Iceland. Intelligent, long living, active and beautiful dogs, easy to maintain. Little exercise and space is required. Behave very well with children, but barks a lot.

Colour: White, black, brown, cream, light blue, orange; whole coloured dogs should be free from white or black markings (free from coloured patches)

Adult height, weight and life expectancy: 15-22 cm, 1.5-3.5 Kg, 11-13 years

Hair coat and grooming requirement: Inner coat: soft, small and silky; outer coat: long, straight and harsh. Hairs are dense in neck, hind limbs and shoulders; require regular grooming.

Caution: Frequent hair shedding and excess tear production is common. During old age check for dental tartar, cataract and kidney problems.

Spitz

Intelligent, active, fearless and frequent barking dog, but easy to manage. Not recognized as pure breed by American or British Kennel Clubs. Difference between Pomeranian and Spitz is confusing. Small Spitz is commonly referred as Pomeranian in India. Likewise, Pomeranian is also sometimes called as miniature Spitz. Originated and developed in many countries including Japan and Germany. German Spitz is the largest in body size. Characteristic features are pointed muzzle, small, pointed, mobile ears and curled fox like tail. Not good for strangers, but behaves well with children. Little exercise and space is required.

Colour: White, black, white and brown, chocolate, red or a combination thereof

Adult height, weight and life expectancy: 40-55 cm, 8-15 Kg, 10-12 years

Hair coat and grooming requirement: Similar to Pomeranian

Caution: Similar to Pomeranian

Mongrel

Non-descript breed found throughout India. Compact, clean body. Clever, active and hardy breed. Good as farm/ guard dog. May roam aimless. Easy to maintain and resistant to many diseases. Highly variable in nature and behaviour.

Colour: Black, white, red, tan and or in a combination thereof

Adult height, weight and life expectancy: 50-60 cm, 20-30 Kg, 11-12 years

Hair coat and grooming requirement: Hairs short and coarse; little grooming is required.

Caution: Some may be aggressive, particularly when not properly socialized or given excess meat in diet.

Bhutia Sheep-dog

Types: Small (known as Bully) and Large

Strong, muscular, compact body with thick hairy tail. Originated in Himalayan region and good for cold environment. Not good for strangers and children.

Colour: Black, black and white, brownish extremities and nose

Adult height, weight and life expectancy: Small: 30-40 cm; 3-10 Kg; Large: 60-70 cm; 15-30 Kg; 10-12 years

Hair coat and grooming requirement: Long hairs, rough and coarse; regular grooming required.

Caution: Some may be furious in nature.

❑❑❑

Chapter 3

Sense Perception, Normal Psychology and Behaviour

The dog is essentially a pack animal that evolved from wolves that are hunter and scavenger by nature. Sense organs developed accordingly to suit their lifestyle in wild. Among senses of sight, smell, touch, hearing and taste, first four in dogs are well developed or even much advanced than human beings.

Sight

Dog's eye-sight, in general, is excellent. They can appreciate even slight movement of any object or prey. In hunting and game breeds, eyes are laterally situated that provide excellent peripheral vision. In some small and toy breeds, eyes are frontally placed and provide excellent binocular vision, but poor close vision.

Smell

Smell is the most developed and most important sense perception in dogs. With large moist surface area of nose, dog can smell any odour from afar.

Touch

A passionate touch and caress by owner or any person is the most pleasant experience for dogs and especially pups. Playing, huddling, licking and pawing, all involve touch perception and are essentially a part of canine behaviour.

Hearing

Hearing is well developed in breeds with erect ears, like German Shepherd and Basenji. Dogs with loose and big ear flap (pinna) have relatively low hearing capacity, but still better than human beings.

Taste

Taste is poorly developed in dogs since they have fewer taste buds in comparison to human beings. This is an adaptation since dog is a scavenger animal and hence can eat things with poor taste. This is why flavour is more important than taste in dog feeding. Warm foods with strong smell are more palatable than a cool spicy food that have little smell but rich in taste.

Besides the senses mentioned above, dogs also have electro-magnetic sense which enables them to forecast earthquakes and take refuge in safe places before they actually take place. Dogs can very easily sense mood of the approaching person. They can also correlate one event with the other and can follow time schedule of different household activities related to them and their daily schedule.

Normal Psychology and Behaviour

Dog's psychology and nature have changed a lot from their ancestors, the wild wolves, after long years of domestication and selective breeding. Yet, many things are still common in them, varying only in degree of their expression. All dogs have four types of natural instincts, prey, pack, flight and fight. Prey instinct enables the dog to attack and chase animals of prey, which is an essential requirement for hunting. The pack instinct strengthen human-animal and animal-animal bond. The fight instinct makes them to fight against all forthcoming dangers or enemies, while flight instinct provokes them to escape sensing life in danger because enemies being too strong. With the lapse of time, prey and fight instincts have weakened, while pack and flight have strengthened. The predominating instinct decides the nature which varies with breed and even with individuals within a breed. Guarding dogs like Rottweiller, German-Shepherd, Doberman etc. have very high prey and fight instincts. Companion animals like Labrador, Golden Retrievers etc. have enough pack instinct as they like family life. Males of all breed have prey and fight instinct, while pack and fight instincts predominate in females.

In nature, dogs remain in packs, prey and fight together under leadership of one alpha male or dominant member who also held the responsibility for their safety. A dog in a family also behaves like a pack member and wants to ensure its position (or status). A dominant male or guarding dog may try to dominate at least over certain family members. If you want an obedient and well behaved dog, from very beginning, try to teach that its position is the lowest in the family hierarchy.

Scent or Urine Marking

In natural wildlife, each pack of wolf and dogs has their own territory for free roaming and catching prey. The territory is demarcated with urine or scent marking by male members of the pack. Such marking also gives information regarding whereabouts of any particular member. This habit still continues particularly in male dogs. They try to mark their territory with urine scents particularly when they are brought to a new place because of their nervousness to face or fight other dogs residing in the area.

Scent Signaling

Some dogs are in habit of smelling sex organs of stranger dog just after meeting. This action provides information about sexual and mental status of the other dog. This is a way of greeting a new or strange dog, just like shaking hands by human beings.

Play-fighting

Dogs play fight with each other. This is a part of socialization and learning process for pups. A pup learns what is right and what is wrong while playing with other puppies and mother. For example, for a wrong action like biting, pup is punished instantaneously by the mother. A dog may also show dominant behaviour while playing with other dogs.

Dominant or Submissive Behaviour

A dog, like human being, may show dominant or submissive behaviour. A dominant dog stares and maintains direct eye contact, approaches slowly but steadily and is ready to bark or attack. Tail is held high and ears remain erect. On the other hand, a submissive dog avoids aggressive fight. In case of confrontation with any dominant dog, it tries to maintain a distance, lowers down its hind legs, and tail is bowed down in-between hind legs. They try to escape away and in case of close approach by a dominant dog or man, lay down on back showing belly by rising hind quarters. Ears are flattened and tail is kept inside hind legs.

❑❑❑

Chapter 4

Initial Care of a Pup

Housing and Care

The ideal time for weaning a pup and bringing home is six to eight weeks of age, just after first deworming and vaccination. Before bringing a new pup home, one should make arrangements for its accommodation and maintenance. It comprises procuring certain things like dog cage, bowls for food and water, collar, lead and soft toys. A cardboard box, after cutting its front-side open, can be used for housing a pup. A small part of the bottom area should be covered with old newspapers, the space provided for soiling. Rest area should have soft bedding, like a piece of blanket. Water bowl should be placed in the area covered by old newspaper and drinking water should be available all the time.

For first few nights, a pup may feel loneliness and try to explore the new surroundings by moving here and there, smelling and licking all the things coming in the way. It may cry when all members of the family have gone to sleep and no one is left for playing or paying attention to it. Close watch on its activities is required during this period and if possible, keep the pup cage/box in your bedroom during initial days. Do not punish the pup for crying; just wait till it calms down. Movement of the pup, when no one is available for watching its actions, can be restricted by providing temporary boundary around the cage/box. Pup chews or licks anything coming across, so avoid keeping harmful things within its reach.

Care During Winter

If you are bringing up pups during winter, special attention should be given towards environmental temperature. A pup must be protected from environmental cold. The body heat generated by mother and other pups keeps a pup warm; so a pup being separated from mother may fall victim of cold exposure and starts coughing, vomiting or passing loose motion. Comfort zone for a pup falls in between 28 to 30°C. Hot clothing for pups is commercially available or can be tailored at home. Some artificial source of heat, like hanging a 60 watt electrical bulb or a room-heater must be provided. If you are using any electrical instrument, make sure that wire cable is beyond reach of the pup.

Feeding

As proper feeding is a very important aspect of healthy up bringing of a pup, it is given in detail in nutrition and feeding chapter.

Toilet Training

After each feeding or just before going to sleep, take the dog out of its cage to a fixed place where it can defecate and urinate. Praise the pup if your attempt is successful. Gradually, it will become a habit of the pup and will stop soiling inside the box/cage. The diet being given is sufficient or not, can be judged on the basis of puppy's health status and growth rate. During the first 5 months, pups grow rapidly and their body weight increases @ 2 to 4 gram/day/kg of their adult body weight. For example, a Labrador pup (body weight of adult dog approx 25 kg), should gain weight @ 50 to 100 gram per day during the first 5 months. Thereafter, the growth rate (and hence weight gain per day) declines and a dog acquires adult body weight by 9 to 12 months of age in small breeds and by 12 to 18 months in large breeds. Remember, birth weight of puppies varies between 120 to 550 gm, depending upon the breed.

Hygiene and Health care

Pups, like human baby, are susceptible to many ailments. Therefore, special attention should be given to hygiene. Bedding and clothings should be changed regularly, washed and dried in the sun when it starts emitting foul smell. Giving frequent bath to pup is not advisable. Over or mal handling, specially by children should be avoided. A sick or even apparently a healthy pup can also transmit many diseases to your baby. Likewise, a sick baby can also transmit certain infections to a pup. Therefore, avoid the contact if any one of them is sick. Soft toys should be available all the time. A pup is usually in the habit of chewing all the objects available for playing. Do not annoy or consider it abnormal. This habit will gradually disappear with age. Mild itching, hair loss and one or two small pustules in the belly develops sometimes despite adopting all hygienic precautions. Do not be panicky until it is accompanied with some other abnormalities such as lack of appetite, dullness, nasal discharge, vomiton, diarrhea, hair loss in patches or foul smelling hair coat.

Play and Exercise

Play and exercise are very important for physical as well as mental development of the pup. Right from early days, provide them toys of suitable size. If there are no children or adult to play with the pup, toys become more essential. A pup living in isolation and boredom during 6 to 14 weeks of age can never become a good dog. Different types of pet toys are available in the market. Purchase a non-toxic toy that does not have any sharp point or separable part that can be chewed and swallowed. Size of the toy should be large enough to make swallowing impossible. A pup during teeth eruption will enjoy chewing toys since it gives some kind of relief from pain and abnormal sensation that supervenes during that period. A tennis ball, foot ball or nylon bones or soft rubber toys are ideal one. Never give small balls or plastic balls, since they can slip inside mouth and throat and induce suffocation. If the pup has to live alone in the house, put a radio or music system on, the sound generated will minimize the anxiety. A small alarm clock, wrapped inside a cloth piece placed beneath the bedding of pup can help a lot during initial weaning days.

❑❑❑

Chapter 5

Housing, Bedding, Collar and Lead

Housing and bedding are essential requirements for dogs. This aspect must be explored before deciding to keep a pet. A pup requires little housing space, but good bedding. Housing and bedding requirements changes with age and season. Collar and lead are essential tools for proper control and training. In this chapter these aspects will be discussed in brief.

Housing

Usually no separate housing is required for one or two small to medium sized dogs. Provide a space in a corner of the house. A small wooden box or a cardboard box with front side open can be placed that serves as a good retiring room. The dog should be trained to use it during leisure time. Children in the house should be asked not to disturb the dog while taking rest. Separate housing is required when large sporting or guarding dogs more than 2 in number are to be kept. Special house for dogs is called as 'kennel'. Dogs should be housed in individual pens (fenced area). The kennel should be well ventilated and constructed in such a way that sufficient day light can enter. The floor should be cemented and well designed and labeled for easy water draining. The floor space of each pen should be sufficient to allow sleeping, and free movement of the dog. Average floor space requirement is 0.75 to 1 square meter for a small size dog; 1-1.25 square meter for a medium size dog and 2 to 2.5 square meter for a large size dog. The pregnant bitch requires double floor space than that required by a male or non-pregnant bitch of same size. The height of walls of pen should be 1 to 1.5 meter. Front door can be made up of metallic frame fitted with wire net. Leave sufficient space between two rows of pens in the kennel. This area should have proper facilities of draining. The size of kennel will depend upon number of pens to be constructed.

Bedding

During summer and rainy days, no special bedding is required. But when ambient temperature is low, provide a piece of old blanket, khadi duster, bed-sheet or rug or old newspapers or mattress. Bedding material should be always non-toxic and non-edible. In villages, dry grass or straw can be used as bedding material. Saw-dust, wood shavings and jute bags can also be used. Bedding material should be dried regularly under sun rays to prevent foul smelling. Change it if torn, damaged or too much soiled. Clean it either by vacuum cleaner or by washing. Bedding material also provides space for hiding ectoparasites, growth of yeast, molds and bacteria. Therefore, maintenance of proper hygiene is essential.

Collar

Collars and leads are essential for pet dogs. Even if not in regular use, they can be required on certain occasions. Collar provides point of attachment for lead and identity tag and is a symbol of a pet animal.

Several types of collars and leads are available in the market. Usually a 12 mm wide collar is suitable for most dogs, particularly for short height, light weight or short necked dog. However, for a large or heavy breed or breeds with long or hairy heck, 2.5 to 4 Cm wide collars are better. A collar may be made up of nylon, leather, steel, rope or thick cloth (denim). Their cost, strength, durability and cleaning requirement vary. Choose a collar according to the need and cost after enquiring details from the shopkeeper. Collar should be put on a pup in about 8-12 weeks of age. Initially it may resist, but will adjust soon. Collars with adjustable length are better for pups and young dogs, since their width can be adjusted according to the requirement. Do not apply neck collar too tight or too loose. It should not slip out of the neck when the dog drags behind. At the same time, it should be loose enough to allow at least two fingers to pass below. It is always better to put an identity tag attached with the neck collar. It may be helpful in cases of accidents, theft or missing.

Lead

Different kind of leads available in the market vary in length, material, cost and strength. Nylon leads are strong, easily washable, cheap and durable. Metallic lead is required for strong/heavy dogs or those who are in habit of chewing the lead. Leather leads are durable and look beautiful. Rope leads are cheap and washable but poor in tensile strength. Lead should be used on regular basis after the pup attains 3 months of age. Let the pup walk freely bearing collar and lead for some time daily under careful observation to avoid any accidents. Gradually, it will adjust.

❑❑❑

Chapter 6

Nutrition and Feeding

Balanced diet is the most important component for growth and maintenance of a healthy body. Formulation of a balanced diet for a dog requires basic knowledge about its nutritional requirement that varies with age, physiological status, environmental conditions, health status etc. Plethora of literature is available on this topic. But after their careful study, you may get confused at the end. In this chapter, attempts have been made to explain nutrition and feeding of dog in a simple and lucid way.

Dogs are classified as carnivores (meat eaters). But, during domestication, they have been adopted to survive on a variety of foods. Now, they can be better classified as omnivores. Almost all the dog breeds, particularly medium and small sized can be even maintained entirely on vegetarian diet. Basic nutrients for dogs can be broadly categorized into protein, fat, carbohydrate, vitamins and minerals. Requirement of individual nutrient varies with breed, age, stage of life, level of activity, housing conditions, and season. During growth, pregnancy and lactation, extra supplementation is required in addition to daily maintenance requirements.

Protein

Protein is required for growth and tissue repair. Dog food should contain at-least 18 to 22% crude protein on dry matter basis. Digestibility of different protein sources varies. In general, animal protein sources, such as egg (100%), meat and fish (90 to 95%) have better digestibility than vegetarian protein sources (60 to 80%) like paneer, pulses, milk, curd, soybean etc. It is always advisable to use a mixture of two or three types of pulses or other protein sources. This practice increases digestibility and bioavailability of different amino-acids present in the protein source.

Fat

Fat is required for energy, growth, reproduction and maintenance of healthy skin and hair-coat. Dog maintained on low fat diet often shows itching, or dry lusterless coat with excess dandruff. Dog food should contain 5 to 8% fat on dry matter basis. Fat is a rich source of energy, increases palatability of the food and helps in metabolism of fat soluble vitamins like A, D, E and K. Rich fat sources are soyabean oil, other vegetable oil, hydrogenated vegetable oil, ghee, poultry and other meat fats. In general, natural fat found in liquid form (with more unsaturated fatty acids) is better than those found in solid form (with more percentage of saturated fatty acids). Fat is nearly 100% digestible, but should not be given in excess in fatty dogs, old dogs or when dog is passing loose stool or suffering from pancreatic or liver diseases. Fat percentage in diet should be increased in dogs recovering from sickness or taking only small quantity of food.

Carbohydrate

Carbohydrate includes starch and sugars that provide about 50% of the total energy requirement of the dog. Ordinary sugar (sucrose) is easily digested by dogs, but milk sugar (lactose) is well tolerated only in pup and young dogs. In few adult dogs, lactose (and hence milk) may cause chronic mild diarrhea. Corn, rice, barley, wheat and other cereal grains are rich in starch and easily digested by dogs.

Maintenance energy requirement varies with body weight and physiological status (Table 1 and 2). Energy requirement is high in a growing pup, pregnant and lactating bitch and dog with high level of physical activities, like those involved in hunting or police duty. It decreases in dogs after 5 to 7 years of age, after removal of testicles or ovary and also in those given limited exercise or remain closely confined.

Table 1 : Total energy requirement of a dog

Body weight (Kg)	Energy requirement (K Cal per day)
2	230
5	450
10	750
15	1010
20	1250
25	1470
30	1675
35	1875
40	2070

Table 2 : Increase in total energy requirement during different physiological status

Physiological status	Increase in energy requirement
Growing pups	2 to 2.5 times
Pregnant bitch (> 6 weeks of pregnancy)	1.5 times
Lactating bitch	3 to 4 times

Vitamin

Vitamins play a crucial role in dog nutrition. They can be broadly classified into two groups; water soluble and fat soluble vitamins. vitamin B complex and vitamin C are major water soluble vitamins. They require frequent intake since they are poorly stored in the body as excess is lost through urine. Excess supplementation of water soluble vitamins rarely causes toxicity. Vitamin B complex is essential for energy metabolism and many enzymatic functions that regulate blood synthesis and functions of nervous and immune system. Supplementation of B complex is required during loss of appetite (anorexia), diarrhea, nervous, renal and hepatic disorders. Fruits, green vegetables, milk and meat products are rich sources of vitamin B complex. There is no dietary requirement for vitamin C because it is synthesized in its body from glucose. However, during sickness extra supplementation may hasten recovery, especially in conditions like bloody diarrhea or blood in urine. Citrus fruits and green vegetables are rich sources of vitamin C. Vitamin A, D, E and K are fat soluble vitamins. They are stored in the body; hence excess supplementation may be harmful. Their requirement, important functions and dietary sources are given in the Table 3.

Table 3 : Fat soluble vitamins

Vitamin	Functions	Daily requirement	Rich natural sources
Vitamin A	Fertility, vision, immune function, maintenance of mucosal surfaces and appetite	5000-25000 IU/ Kg/ day	Liver, fish liver oils, dairy products, egg, green vegetables
Vitamin D	Skeletal (Bone) growth, Ca and P metabolism, maintenance of appetite	500-5000 IU/ Kg/ day	Fish liver oil, dairy products, natural sunlight
Vitamin E	Maintenance of fertility and muscle mass	50-1000 IU/ Kg/ day	Vegetable oils, meat, vegetables, fish liver oil
Vitamin K	Blood clotting	-	Egg, leafy vegetables

Mineral

Twelve minerals are essential for dogs, viz. Ca, P, Mg, K, Na, Cl, Fe, Cu, Mn, Zn, I and Se. Among them, calcium (Ca) and phosphorus (P) are the most important from nutrition point of view. Deficiency or excess, both are harmful and can cause clinical diseases. In diet, ideal ratio of Ca and P should be 1.2 to 1.4: 1. Diet poor in Ca and P causes rickets (bending of leg bones) in young animals, while excess calcium supplementation may cause zinc deficiency. Sodium (Na), potassium (K) and chloride (Cl) play important role in maintenance of fluid and electrolyte balance in the body. Their estimation and careful supplementation are required in dehydration, vomition, diarrhea, intestinal obstruction, heart failure and renal failure. Copper and iron are important for red blood cell synthesis and their supplementation help in recovery of anemia. Zinc is important for skin and hair coat health. Its deficiency causes hair loss, thickening of skin (parakeratosis) and skin infections (pyoderma). Selenium and Iodine are important for muscle growth and maintenance of fertility.

Fiber

Fiber does not have any nutritional value and is also indigestible. But, it is essential for proper functioning of digestive system. Dog food should contain about 5 % fiber on dry matter basis. Its level should be increased up to 10 to 15% in dogs, suffering from diabetes or obesity. Fiber absorbs toxins present in the digestive system and increases food passage rate. Its importance in food passage can be guessed from the fact that mean transit time of ingested food is approximately 47, 41, 33 and 29 hours in dogs receiving food containing 0.6, 6.5, 11.2 and 14.7% crude fiber, respectively. Dogs suffering from chronic constipation should be given high fiber containing diet. Wheat bran is an easily available rich source of fiber and phosphorus. Green and leafy vegetables and fruits are other good sources of fiber and other nutrients.

Water

Water intake of a dog varies with body weight, type of food, exercise, environmental conditions, and disease conditions leading to fluid or blood loss. A growing pup fed entirely on milk diet may not take water or can only lick occasionally. But dog suffering from vomition, diarrhea, chronic gastritis, kidney problem, diabetes etc. would like to drink at short intervals.

Feeding

Dog can eat all the food of human choice. The spectrum of tasty food is similar or even wider than that of human beings. Small breeds are often selective eaters and fussy, but medium and large breeds will consume even less tasty diet (as judged by you). Changes in food increases palatability, but frequent change is neither needed nor recommended, since it may fail to meet the essential nutritional requirements or may predispose obesity. Too much salt and spices should be avoided. Usually, boiled or baked food with little salt and spice will evoke the hunger. Palatability of warm and freshly prepared food is more than cold one, especially during winters. Spoiled or long stored food should not be offered. At a time, dog should never be given too much and unchecked amount of food. Always offer the quantity that will satisfy only about 80% of the hunger, i.e. it should be able to eat little more if offered. After a careful observation of the abdominal distension (enlargement) after feeding, you will learn how much quantity at a time is sufficient for the dog.

There are three basic questions that arise while planning feeding schedule for a dog, 1. what should be given? (Type of food); 2. how much should be given? (Quantity of food); and 3. When it should be given? (Time of feeding). Answers of all these questions vary mainly with age and physiological status. Therefore, it will be discussed according to different stages of their life.

Pup

A pup should be allowed to suck the mother soon after birth. Intake of colostrum within 12 to 24 hours of birth is essential to acquire passive immunity (disease resistance power) and good survival rate of pups. Up to 3 weeks of age, a pup should have free access to mother's milk and usually no additional food or water is required. Thereafter, pups start licking edibles and may be given boiled milk with little sugar. After 6 weeks, mother's milk is unable to meet their nutritional requirement and hence other edibles should also be given. A teaspoonful of Cerelac or Farex can be added to a cup of diluted milk or water. Giving small quantity of soft food, like Dalia (crushed maize or wheat boiled in milk), Halwa (Freid and boiled suzi or besan), soybean nickets (bari) boiled in milk or water, paneer pieces, egg white (boiled), chicken soup (without spice, with little salt) and fruits like mango, banana, papaya, apple are always advisable. Initially frequent feeding (small quantity given at short time-intervals) may be required, but with advancement of age, frequency of feeding should be reduced (Table 4). The next food should be different from previous one, i.e. you can select 3 to 4 different recipe and serve them alternately. This will ensure balanced nutrition and proper food intake. A pup may defecate soon after feeding. So observe the pup and start toilet training accordingly. Ensure availability of clean drinking water all the time.

Orphan pup

Sometimes either dam (mother) is lost or dam's milk production alone is insufficient to feed all the pups. In such condition, hand feeding is essential to save their lives. Smaller pup requires more care and expertise. They can be fed either with baby milk feeding bottles attached with a nipple or with the help of a dropper. Composition of milk replacement is given in table 5. Individual components can be mixed properly in a clean bottle and can be stored in refrigerator for 2 to 3 days. Alternatively, condensed cow or goat milk can be fed alone, but do not forget to give calcium syrups (5 to 10 drops twice daily) and multivitamin drops (2 to 5 drops twice daily) just after milk feeding. Give small quantity (say 2 to 5 ml) at a time and watch for abdominal distension, interest in food and activities. Slowly you will learn how much quantity is sufficient at a time and what should be frequency of feeding. If diarrhoea develops, either reduce the quantity or frequency of feeding and consult a veterinarian. In the meantime give ORS solution intermittently to avoid dehydration. Maintenance of hygienic feeding and husbandry practices are essential since orphan pups are mostly weak and prone to various diseases.

Table 4 : Feeding schedule for a pup

Age	Feeding frequency	Major ingredients/ food items	Additional supplementation
3 weeks and above	Frequent	Mother's milk, condensed cow milk, goat milk, Cerelac with water, milky porridge	Multivitamin drops, 2 to 4 drops twice daily
6 weeks and above	6 times a day	Condensed cow milk or goat milk, add ½ to 2 tsf Complan/ Farex/ Cerelac to milk or water, hard boiled or scrambled egg with yolk, minced cooked meat or fish (with no bones), chicken soup. Mother's milk can be stopped.	Calcium syrup ½ tsf twice daily, multivitamin drops 2 to 4 drops twice daily
12 weeks and above	5 times a day	Cow/buffalo/ goat milk, dalia, halwa, boiled liver, egg white, paneer pieces, fruits, cooked meat and fish, half-boiled whole egg, chapati, cooked vegetables, rice-curd, rice-pulse, soya chunks (Bari) boiled in milk	Calcium syrup 1 to 2 tsf twice daily, multivitamin drops 5 to10 drops twice daily

Table 5 : Recipe for orphan pup

Constituents	Quantity
Cow milk	800 ml
Cream	200 ml
Egg yolk (yellow)	One
Calcium syrup like Ascal	2 tsf
Multivitamin drops/ syrup like Vimeral	1 ml

Adult dogs

Dogs more than one year old can be maintained on one to two diets per day. It is always advisable to give two diets per day especially when non-veg items are not given. One heavy meal can be given in the morning (around 10 o'clock) and one light diet (half of the morning diet) should be given in the evening (around 6 o'clock). Reverse the schedule for working dogs going for hard work during day time. Working dogs require high fat additives like cheese, butter, soya oil (2 to 3 tsf), ghee and fatty meat to meet the energy requirements. Two homemade diets for adult dogs are given in the table 6. The quantity of each ingredient is sufficient for one meal and not for the entire day. Biscuits can also be prepared at home (Table 7) and given occasionally as reward for good behaviour.

Table 6 : Homemade diets for adult dogs

	Items (in gram)	Body weight of dog			
		8 Kg	10 Kg	15 Kg	20 Kg
Diet I	Wheat flour bread, boiled rice or dalia	140	175	265	350
	Soya oil/ cheese/ butter	10	15	20	25
	Boneless meat/ fish	50	65	100	125
Diet II	Wheat four bread, boiled rice or dalia	100	125	200	250
	Vegetables	150	200	300	400
	Milk	250	300	400	450
	Eggs	one	one	Two	Two

Table 7 : Composition of homemade dog biscuit

Ingredient	Weight (in gm)
Wheat flour	750
Soya-flour	135
Fat/ Ghee	40
Salt	5
Mineral and Vitamin mixture	10
Calcium/ Bone power	60

Pregnant and Lactating bitch

Nutritional requirement increases during pregnancy and lactation. During first month of pregnancy, no special supplementation is required. Only marginal (up to 5%) increase in diet is sufficient. But during second month of pregnancy, foetal growth is maximum and hence increase the diet gradually. Eggs (1 to 2), liver (50 gm), chicken (150 gm), milk, pulses or paneer (50-100 gm) and seasonal fruits should be added daily in the diet. Bitch should be fed two to three times a day during last week of pregnancy. Appetite usually decreases, so small quantity of highly palatable and nutritive diets should be offered frequently.

After whelping, bitch may consume only little food or even go off- fed for one or two days. Thereafter, appetite increases gradually and usually attain a peak by 2 to 3 weeks, the period when milk production is maximum. Food consumption during first month of lactation may be double to that before pregnancy and it may further increase during second month of lactation. Give the food 2 to 3 times a day. Egg, liver, pulses, paneer, meat and fruits should also be given. Calcium syrup (1 to 2 tsf twice daily) and multivitamin supplements, like Seacod, 2 capsules once daily should also be given especially when litter size (total number of pups) is large. After weaning of pups, diet should be gradually reduced to the normal basal diet within a week.

Geriatric dog

Aging starts in dogs after 7 years. Gradually their immunity weakens and the dog become more prone for digestive upsets, arthritis, obesity, dental problems, kidney and liver disorders. Dietary modifications can help to prevent them by delaying undesirable aging. Total caloric requirement of older dogs decreases, but protein requirement do not varies much. Therefore, old dog should be fed with diet low in energy (low fat and up to some extent, low in digestible carbohydrate). Source of high quality proteins (eggs, meat, paneer) should not be reduced, rather their percentage in diet should be increased, if total food intake is low. Antioxidant vitamins (like vitamin E and A) and vitamin B complex should be supplemented regularly. Give periodically Evion (200 or 400 mg) or Seacod capsule (Cod liver oil) after consulting any veterinarian. Give vitamin B complex syrup or liver tonic, if sudden decrease in diet is noticed despite apparently healthy look of the old dog. Give high fiber diet specially if there is any difficulty in passing faeces or mild but chronic constipation is suspected. Calcium syrups are not required until prescribed by any vet. If the dog is suffering from any disease, consult a veterinary doctor for feeding management.

Sick dog

Feeding of sick dogs, especially those suffering from chronic diseases like kidney failure and heart diseases require special care. It should be done under supervision of a veterinarian. Dogs suffering from mild diarrhea can be given boiled rice with curd, paneer, boiled egg white, boiled potatoes etc. Dogs with severe diarrhea or frequent vomition should be fed only after recommendation of a veterinary doctor. In the mean time ORS solution or a mixture of glucose and Electral powder with water can be given.

Liver diseases

Carbohydrate rich diet should be provided to dogs suffering from liver diseases. Excess fat and salt in diet should be avoided. Lean meat, paneer, curd or pulses mixed with rice can be given. Corn flex along with milk or curd is also good. Fruits and vegetables should be given on regular basis. Multivitamin syrups containing vitamin A, D, E, K and Choline can help early recovery from the disease.

Kidney diseases

Low protein, high carbohydrate diet should be given to kidney patients. Salt should not be added in the diet; potassium and phosphorus rich diet should be avoided. High quality protein sources like boiled eggs, chicken soup, milk, curd etc. can be given, but not in excess.

Obesity

In obesity, dogs should be given diet containing fewer calories with high fiber and protein content. Lean meat, chapatti, vegetables and fruits can be given. Milk sould be mixed with water to increase the bulk and volume. Slowly decrease the quantity of the diet up to 20 per cent of the initial one, but care should also be taken to avoid nutritional deficiencies.

Points to remember

1. Always give the food at a particular time and place in same utensils.
2. Food should be preferably fresh, moist and warm. To evoke hunger, scent of the food is more important than taste. Left over food should not be served second time.
3. Always offer food less than the quantity to fully satisfy the hunger of a dog. It is better to give small quantity frequently, rather than huge quantity at a time.
4. Small breed dog can be easily maintained on complete vegetarian diet. However, large breed dogs often suffer from nutritional deficiency when maintained on only veg diet. Meat or egg should be served occasionally for better growth and health. Remember, flavor of meat or egg increases the palatability.
5. Following consumption of meat, paneer or other protein or fat rich diet in excess, the dog may not show interest in food for few days. Dog may even vomit once or twice to relieve the gastric discomfort. It is natural, so do not worry. You can give some antacids or digestive stimulants after consulting a vet.
6. Any change in food or feeding schedule should be gradual.
7. During breeding season, male dogs may go off-fed and become restless in attempt to discover mating partner. It is a natural phenomenon, so do not worry.
8. Decrease/loss of appetite without any obvious reason is a sign that may be due to a variety of disease conditions. So consult the doctor immediately.

Do not give following food items

1. *Excess chocolates since it can promote obesity*. Moreover, it may contain theobromide that can be toxic for the dog.
2. *Grapes*: Excess grapes may cause acute kidney failure.
3. *Chicken and fish with bones*: Dogs may ingest sharp bones that may be dangerous.
4. *Excess fast food*: It promote obesity and digestive problems.

□□□

Chapter 7 Grooming and Bathing

Grooming

Daily grooming is essential especially for breeds with long hair coat like Cocker Spaniel, Pekingese, Afghan Hound *etc.* Grooming increases blood circulation to hair follicles. It also prevents excessive hair loss, formation of hair mats and tangles. Grooming is usually carried out in two stages, first combing and then brushing or wiping. Equipments required include combs of different sizes, wide toothed comb, fine comb, bristle brush, duster and scissors.

Combing

Combing should be started from the head and then moving towards the back. In long hair coat breeds, use wide-toothed comb with teeth about 2 mm apart from each other. The length of teeth should be sufficient to cross through hair and reach the body surface. Push the comb into the hair coat, move towards the direction of hairs and finally give only slight twist against their natural growth. In long hair breeds, go for combing with small strokes. Fine combs can be used in medium and short coat breeds. Avoid using combs that generate much friction and charges. Their use may cause hair loss.

Special attention should be given towards hairs present over head, eyes, hind quarters and tail. Trim them if overgrown and causing any problem.

Brushing

After combing a bristle brush is applied which helps removing fallen, damaged and broken hairs. This gives final touch to combing. Brush is applied in a similar way as the comb. Long, less dense bristle should be used for long hair breeds; while short, dense-bristle brush is better for short hair breeds. In place of brush, duster can be used after combing in short-hair dogs. A cotton or khadi duster is better than a synthetic one.

Bathing

When to bath?

Frequent/daily bath is harmful for skin and hair coat of dogs. Frequency of bath depends upon season, dog hygiene and presence of any skin or hair coat problem. During summer, dog should be given a bath after an interval of one or two weeks; while bath at every 3 to 4 weeks interval will suffice during winters and rainy seasons. Frequency may be increased when hair coat starts smelling foul or is infected. On the other hand, too frequent bath may induce skin problems like itching, excess hair loss, lusterless, dry and brittle hair. During winter, a pup should be given bath only when surrounding temperature is within the comfort zone, otherwise it may catch cold and nasal discharge or diarrhea may follow. To avoid cold exposure, either use warm water or only wipe out the body with a towel soaked with diluted mild disinfectants like savlon or dettol.

How to bath?

One can bathe a dog in a bath-tub or any place with pakka floor. Someone should hold the dog and then cotton plugs be inserted in the openings of ears. Wetting its body should start from the back. One can use a shower attachment or slow running tap water or a jug filled with water. As soon as water is poured on the head, the dog starts shaking its head and other parts of the body.

Apply soap or shampoo first on the rear parts, then on neck and finally on the head. Rub it thoroughly on the whole body. After applying medicated soaps/shampoos, one should wait at least for 5 minutes to allow it to work. Then start rinsing, first the head region and then progressing towards backward direction. Rinse properly so that soap/shampoo is completely washed out. During winter, allow for few minutes to stand under sun so that hair coat becomes dry. During rainy season towel your dog and let it dry in some warm place. Hair dryers may also be used, but with caution since dog may frighten and jump due to unusual sound or sensation. Remember, fungal infection may set up if hair coat remain wet for long time. Pinna (External ears) and ear opening should be dried with the help of soft cloth folded over index finger. Cotton plug, should be then removed.

Table 1 : Different shampoos and soaps for dogs

Group	Purpose/ Condition	Commercial products	
I	For routine use (healthy and shiny hair coat)	Shampoo	Notix green, Arnibax, Samglow PV
		Soap	Petmosole, Notix green, Boww, Samglow
II	When louse, fleas, ticks and mites are present	Shampoo	Cizaflux, Furfree, Notix scrub, Tikkil
		Soap	Furfree, Clinar-M, Cizabath, Softas
III	When excess dandruff is present	Shampoo	Seledruff, Selson
IV	When fungal infection is suspected	Shampoo	Sheen-n-Kleen forte, Micodin, Myconil
V	When excessive itching is present or hair coat is foul smelling/ greasy	Shampoo	Petben, Sulphoben, Ichgon

Note : All other products except group I should be used only after consulting a vet. Avoid using Group II products when large, open wound or generalized bruises are present or dog is sick or pup is below 3 months of age. Follow the instructions written on leaflets or containers of the products.

Which shampoo or soap should be used?

Many owners think that shampoo or soap intended for human use can also be used for dog. But this is a wrong assumption. Dog skin differs from our skin in many ways. Human skin is acidic in nature (pH about 5.5) while dog's skin is alkaline (pH about 7.5). Human skin is comparatively thicker and consists of about 10 to 15 layers; but there are only 3 to 5 layers in dog's skin. Hair follicles grow continuously in human, but the growth is cyclic in dogs. Thinner epidermis, quicker turn over rate of hair follicles and dense hair coat leading to poor ventilation make the dog's skin more prone to various infections. Therefore, special dog shampoo and soap manufactured by any good company is better for routine use. But be careful before using any product manufactured by local companies, as they may harm your dog's skin and hair coat. Carbolic soaps or dettol should be avoided and no medicated products should be used on routine basis. You can choose a suitable shampoo or soap with the help of the Table 1.

□□□

Chapter 8

Care of Teeth, Eye, Ear and Nail

Teeth

Like human beings, dogs have two sets of teeth, deciduous (temporary) and permanent teeth. Pups have 28 deciduous teeth while adults have 42 permanent teeth. In puppies, the deciduous teeth begin to erupt at about 3-4 weeks of age and by the age of 3 to 4 months, their replacement with permanent teeth starts. Dog becomes full mouth with all permanent teeth (total 42) by the age of 6 months. Tooth is of four types, incisor, canine, premolar and molar.

Dental problems are more common in older dogs. Regular check up and cleaning can help preventing dental problems, although vet assistance may be essential on some occasions as described below:

1. *Persisting temporary tooth*: Usually the temporary tooth is lost before eruption of the permanent teeth. But sometimes, eruption of permanent tooth occurs before loss of the temporary one. The persisting temporary tooth may create problem and disturb the normal dental alignment. The problem is more common in small breeds, where incisor and canine teeth are mostly involved.

2. *Plaque and calculus (tartar) formation*: Plaque is deposition of sticky yellow to tan coloured material on the tooth. When becomes hard after mineralization, it is called as calculus or tartar. Tartar removal is essential; otherwise infection in gum may set up, resulting loose tooth that falls easily and early. Tartar removal is essentially a job of veterinarian, who performs it under anaesthesia.
3. *Gingivitis*: It is inflammation of the gum (gingiva). Gum appears swollen, red, may bleed and give foul smell. Ropy salivation starts and the dog refuses to eat. Use of antibiotics and anti-inflammatory/pain killers are recommended.
4. *Dental caries*: Dental caries are less common in dogs because their diet contains less carbohydrate resulting lower population of carbohydrate fermenting bacteria in normal oral flora.

Dental care tips

- Dogs should be provided soft toys or chewing objects, like synthetic bones. Give fruits and hard biscuits to encourage chewing. This practice reduces tartar formation. Specially formulated diets are available in the foreign countries that significantly reduce dental plaques after about 6 months of their use.
- Regular tooth brushing is difficult to follow but is very helpful in preventing dental problems. Dog will accept tooth brushing if they are trained since young age. First train the dog for head, face and lip handling. Gently stroke the face and muzzle and try to lift the lips while keeping the mouth closed. This procedure is repeated patiently for few days until the dog becomes accustomed. Then gradually introduce brushing. Toothbrushes available for human can be used in dogs. But, human toothpastes should not be used since they generate excess foam and usually the dog dislikes their taste. Veterinary dentifrice gels and pastes containing zinc-ascorbate, chlorhexidine or fluoride should be used in dogs. Teeth are cleaned by rotating the brush in a circular motion after placing it at a 45-degree angle over the teeth. Wash the teeth and mouth by pouring water through a syringe or spray gun.

Eye

Examine the eyes regularly for presence of any discharge (watery or thick creamy), swelling, excessive redness or haziness, opacities, third eye lid prolapse or abnormal tissue out growth. Normal eyes are shiny with outer surface (cornea and sclera) moist and smooth. If any trauma to eyeball occurs or outer eye surface appears dry or uneven (corneal ulcers?) immediate medical attention is required; otherwise permanent damage can occur. Eye problems and accidental eye damages are quite common in breeds with protruding eyes, such as Pekingese, Pug, French Bull Dog etc. Eye drops intended for human use should never be used without consulting a vet, since corticosteroids or some other ingredients may even harm sometimes (in corneal ulcers). Any discharge present in corners of the eye should be cleaned gently with the help of a cotton swab soaked with luke-warm water or any eye cleansing solution. Tear duct occlusion, inflammation and continuous irritation caused by hairs or eye lashes or foreign body and glaucoma are common causes of excessive tear production. Tear may wet and stain the hairs present around the eyes promoting microbial growth and infection. Partial or complete blindness in dogs is often recognized late because the dog often manages routine work and movement in familiar places with the help of memory and hearing. If any doubt about weak eye sight arises, allow the dog to move in a new area and watch its movements (whether it collides with obstacles or walk smoothly?). Weak eye sight may be associated with retinal degeneration or detachment or some other problems; many of them are genetically controlled. Cataract is another reason particularly in old dogs, and it may not be possible to treat the condition. Only antioxidant vitamins and minerals are given to slow down the development and maturity of the catract.

Ear

Ear of dog can be divided into three parts, outer ear (pinna or ear flap and ear canal), middle ear (ear drum, tympanic caviety and ossicles) and inner ear (auditory nerves and semicircular canals). Structure of pinna varies with breed, but the structure of middle and inner ear remains same. Dogs with pendulous pinna (Spaniels, Basset etc.), excess hairs on pinna (Spaniels) and narrow ear canal (Poodles) are more prone for ear problems. Infection usually starts from outer ear, spreading into middle and inner ear. Therefore, regular ear examination (at monthly interval) and early treatment can reduce severity of the problem.

Ear examination: Restrain the dog and lift the ear flap. Look into ear canal, if required, use torch light. If excess hairs are coming in the way, clip them carefully with scissors. Normal ear canal is lined by smooth hairless skin coated with a little wax. Healthy ear smells waxy. But putrefied or foul smell suggests infection. Presence of excess wax, discharge and swelling or pain reflex while ear handling suggest ear problem. Head tilting, head shaking, ear scratching, hearing loss (deafness), and repeated pawing at the ears are some other signs of ear problem. Consult a doctor immediately, if any of the above signs are present.

Ear cleaning: Clip excess hairs present on inner side of the pinna and around ear canal opening. They impair ventilation and promote bacterial, fungal and mite growth. Sometimes, dead or fallen hairs along with excess wax and dirt make a plug like structure that blocks the ear canal. Clean it carefully with fingers or cotton swab or bud (available for human use). But, never poke a cotton bud too deep into ears; otherwise you may push the debris or foreign body deep into the ear.

If excess wax or dry material is present coating ear canal, pour few drops of warm liquid paraffin or glycerin or olive oil or coconut oil or any ear cleansing solution using a dropper (as described in medication section). Rub base of the pinna with fingers. After few minutes, take a ear bud, hold it like a pencil close to cotton plug and clean the material. Clean all the material by changing the buds.

Nail

Pups have sharp nails. They may induce injury to eye, ears and other body parts while scratching with legs. Clip the nails in such cases using human nail clipper or small size dog nail clipper. Nails of dog grow continuously, but are usually self-trimmed by friction during usual movement on hard and rough ground. Dog given plenty of exercise, therefore, rarely requires nail trimming. However, nails of the dog housed indoor or exercised on soft ground like garden only may overgrow in a circular fashion causing injury to food pad and pain during movement. Nails colliding with ground and producing typical sounds during movement is indicative of overgrown nails. Trim such nails immediately. Special dog nail trimmers or clippers are available in the market. The pink area inside the nail contains blood and nerve supply and is called as quick or nail-bed. Nail should be trimmed always leaving the quick area; otherwise bleeding and excess pain supervene. In case of accidental bleeding, take a wet cotton swab, put few potassium permanganate crystals over it and apply on the bleeding area. Bleeding will be stopped immediately. Consult the vet for further treatment.

❑❑❑

Chapter 9

Training and Exercise

Training is essential to inculcate discipline and good manners in a dog. Like a human child, necessary manners must be taught to a pup right from early days. An untrained dog may be a social threat, or sometimes, a matter of embarrassment for the owner. But, keeping a properly trained dog is a status symbol and can serve many useful purposes. Moreover, a dog trained from early days usually remains free from many bad habits like chasing and barking at strangers or newcomers to the house, food-begging and rude or dominant behaviour.

Informal training start from the day pup enters in the house. The ideal age for bringing a pup home is 6 to 8 weeks, when deworming and vaccination are underway. A good mother and healthy pup-mates are the best teachers, from whom a pup learns basic principles of social behaviour. A pup separated from them at an early age is more prone for developing bad habits and catching deadly infections.

Name recognition

A pup must be given a good name. The name should be simple, short and maximum up to five or six alphabets in length. It should be different from the name of preexisting pup or dog in the house, and common commands like come, go, stay, heel, down, no, hold, good, bad etc (See Chapter 30). Name recognition should be the first lesson for the pup. The best time to teach is just before feeding. Call the name again and again before a pup arrives near the feeding place. All the family members should call the pup by the same name; otherwise the pup may get confused. Usually the pup starts recognizing its name within one or two weeks after arrival.

House-breaking or toilet training

Dogs usually do not soil their sleeping area and prefer to urinate or defecate at specific places. Pups like clean, dry and thermo-comfortable living area. But if toilet-training is not given, a pup may answer the nature's call at different places, thus making the house dirty. Toilet training is therefore essential from hygienic point of view.

Pup urinates and defecates after every session of eating, drinking and playing. Sniffing the ground, moving in a circle and lowering hind quarters are signs, indicating that it is going to answer the nature's call within next few seconds. Quickly pick up the pup and place it on a sheet of old newspapers. An old piece of soiled newspaper (of previous session) should also be placed on it. Scent of its own urine and faeces acts as a stimulant and helps the pup to decide the right place for defecation. Praise the pup soon after it finishes the job. After every meal and sleeping session or few hours interval, take the pup in the same area for defecation and urination. The area should not be far away from the living area, since a pup cannot hold on nature's call for long time. First call the pup by name and move slowly in backward direction towards the destination, where old newspaper is kept for toilet. After arrival, the pup may sniff or play for some time and then finishes the job. Give the command "finish" as soon as it starts the process. Later on, the command "finish" when given at the right time, acts as a stimulus for urination or defecation. In case pup starts answering nature's call at wrong place, repeat the command "no" again and again and quickly bring the pup at some other place. Do not loose temper if it soils the wrong place despite your all efforts. Clean the area and apply diluted vinegar or some strong smelling disinfectant that can hide the smell of urine or faeces. If smell persists, pup may again use the place as toilet. Usually a pup is accustomed to the paper toilet in one to two weeks. Gradually train the pup to relieve outside the house at certain fixed place, like corner of a garden or some other remote area. Older dogs can be trained to defecate once or twice a day during morning or evening walking or exercise session.

The dog trainer

It is a general belief that only a professional dog trainer can train a dog properly. This notion is totally wrong. Basic obedience training can be given by any dog owner who loves the dog, has leisure time and knows the basics of dog training. An ideal trainer should be calm, energetic, quick to react and have a lot of patience and ability to assess the animal psychology. His behaviour with dog during training session should be gentle but firm. Consistency is must to achieve good results. Also, all the members of the family should treat the dog in a similar way, not allowing the dog to break the training rules. For a similar action, all family members should react in a similar way. If one praises and allows a dog to perform one action, while others punish for the same, it may be confused totally and the training may go in vein.

Preparing the dog for training

Training should be given preferably at a fixed time in the morning or evening. The pup should not be tired, bored or drowsy. Never give a heavy meal just before a training session. Empty stomach is preferable since the dog will be more active, attentive and enjoy the treat given as reward. Each session should be short, up to 10 minutes for pups and 20 minutes for adults, otherwise they may loose interest in the training. Each session should end up with some pleasant experience. Pup or adult dog should be allowed to play and offered some favourite food at end of the training session.

The right place

The place where the dog feels comfortable and considers his own territory is the most suitable one. There should be minimum distractions like noise, traffic, human or animal population, so that the dog could easily concentrate on training. Any open area in the house is the best place for initial days of training. Once accustomed, training area may be shifted to the nearby park or any other area familiar to the dog. Fenced area is better, since chances of escape or accidents are less.

Requirements

No specific equipments are required for training purposes. The dog must be habitual to wear neck collar and chain while walking.

Normal collar and chain are required for gentle, sensitive and soft natured pup, while choke collar is essential for hardy pup that may refuge to follow the commands. The basic purpose is to ensure full command and control over the dog, whenever required.

Positive and negative enforcement

Positive and negative enforcement are two essential tools for dog training. Positive enforcement includes rewards in terms of either tasty edibles or praise or hugging or patting with love. Initially, every obedient behaviour or action should be followed by some kind of positive enforcement. But gradually reduce their frequency. Treats should not be given too frequently; otherwise, dog's attention may be diverted more towards them.

Negative enforcement can be in terms of verbal command or physical punishment. A stern "no" should be voiced again and again, quickly after any disobedience or undesirable action. Remember, a dog can only understand any action is desirable or not, only if, positive or negative enforcement is given within 5 seconds of that particular action. If time lapse is more, there is no use of any command, reward or punishment. Rather, it will confuse the dog and problem may worsen. Physical punishment should not be given until and unless no other ways left. Gentle striking the dog over the head with a fold of old newspaper or some stick can be tried. Other way is to place the dog in a cage in isolated place for few hours. Negative enforcement should always be used carefully, since dominant dogs of certain breed may become aggressive.

Types of dog training

Basic obedience training: It includes general training for daily activities. It is essential for every dog and should be started at the age of 5 to 6 months. Dogs more than 7 to 9 months old are difficult to train. Basic obedience training includes following commands:

Heel/ Walk on Heel: Purpose of this command is to train the dog for walking with owner or other person in a disciplined way. Apply neck collar and chain or a lead and start walking with the dog. Control the movements of the dog by holding the lead firmly close to its neck, but at a distance, comfortable for both you and the dog. Help the dog to come and move in required position, i.e. dog's right shoulder should be parallel to your left leg. Call "heel" firmly and repeatedly while walking. Keep on repeating the command in a pleasant way. Check any undesirable movements of the dog and say "no" whenever it tries to pull out in forward or backward direction. Say "good boy" or "good baby" when it moves in the desired way. Initially, the training should be given in the area free from activity or vehicular noises or movements of people. Once trained in such area, go for a walk in busy areas.

Sit : After learning walk on heel, the dog should be trained to sit on buttocks, i.e. in typical dog sitting posture. While walking, stop at any quiet place, hold the chain with one hand and gently but firmly press the back just above the pelvis with other hand. While doing so, say repeatedly "Sit". Then again move for some distance, stop for some time and repeat the process. This command can also be taught at the time of feeding. Call the dog for food, but do not offer. After arrival, it will sit while waiting for the food. Repeat the command "sit" several times as soon as it starts sitting down. If it does not sit himself, press the back and give the command. Do not offer food until the act is performed successfully.

Stay : The next assignment for the dog should be to learn "stay" command. After walking for some distance, give the command "sit". Then hold the chain high by raising your right hand and start moving in a circle around the dog in anticlockwise direction. If the dog tries to stand up, give the command "stay" and a gentle but firm jerk to the lead. Visual direction to stay can also be given with other free hand.

Next stage is to teach to "stay" without using a lead. Ask the dog to sit, and then you start moving in backward direction. Stretch your one arm forward keeping the palm upward (like a signal given by traffic police) towards the dog and repeat the command "stay". Keep on moving until you are out of dog's sight. Praise the dog after your return and give some treat.

Wait and Come : The way of teaching the command "wait" is similar to "stay". Command the dog to sit and then ask repeatedly "wait". Hold the lead and move away few meters. Then call the dog name and give the command "come". If it does not come, give a gentle jerk to the lead. When the dog comes close to you, praise him a lot. But never use "come" command to punish the dog, otherwise it may refuse to follow.

Down : This is an extension of "sit" command. After sitting, bow the dog down by moving its front legs with one hand and holding the neck region with other hand. While doing so, keep on repeating "down" command. If the dog maintains the position, praise a lot, but also show your resentment, when it tries to disobey or does not maintain the position.

Besides above commands, some additional commands can also be taught to dogs. They are as follows:

Command	Meaning
Go	Move away from the location
Quiet	To stop barking
Speak/ Bark	To start barking
Hold/ Guard	To hold an object in his possession under the forelimbs in down position or guarding the object by sitting beside.
Fetch	To retrieve any object
Bow and salute	Salute after sitting and raising forearm

Advanced training : Dogs can be trained to perform different tasks like guarding, explosive detection, scent determination, tracking, assisting physically challenged persons etc. Extensive training is required for these purposes and hence is better performed by a professional dog trainer. Their detailed descriptions are beyond the scope of this book.

Exercise

Regular exercise is must for maintenance of health and prevention of obesity. But always remember, an exhaustive exercise or wrong way of exercise may harm and cause musculoskeletal problems. There is no thumb rule how much exercise should be given at a time? Go for maximum up to 15 minutes session initially and increase the duration gradually, if required. All sessions must be followed by a leisure or rest period. Never give rigorous exercise after heavy meals, otherwise stomach or intestine may strangulate creating serious problem. Stop the exercise as soon as the dog looses interest. The need of exercise varies with breed, like small and toy breed require less, while Hounds, Terriers, Retrievers and other large breeds require more. Morning and evening walk is a good exercise and may also be suitable for your daily routine. If children are there, allow them to play with dog during evening hours. Dogs really enjoy their company.

❑❑❑

Chapter 10

Endoparasites and Deworming

Pups and adult dogs frequently suffer from gastrointestinal worms (endoparasites). Milk of the infected bitch (mother) and contaminated surroundings containing eggs or larva of parasites are two major sources of infection. Pups and young dogs are habitual to explore the environment by licking and chewing, and during this process, they may pick up infection.

Common endoparasites of a dog can be broadly classified into two groups, round worms and flat worms (tape worms).

Round worms

Ascarid worms (Toxocara) and hook worms (Ancylostoma) are two most important round worms of the dog. Pups may get Toxocara infection soon after birth by sucking milk containing larva of the parasite. Later on, larva become adult and cause reduced appetite, rough hair coat, poor growth and pot bellied appearance. Diarrhoea or constipation, vomition and increased or depraved appetite may also be observed.

Hook worms are more harmful than ascarid worms and can cause serious illness even in adult dogs. The eggs and larva of hook worms are highly active and resistant to adverse climatic conditions. They can penetrate even intact mucosa and skin to cause infection. Infected dog shows signs of loose tarry faeces (Black/coffee coloured, due to presence of digested blood), or bloody diarrhea, weakness, vomition, dehydration, and shock. Death may occur in untreated cases. If infection is mild or dog is hardy, anemia, weight loss and lethargy may only be observed.

Diagnosis of round worms is based upon clinical symptoms and microscopic examination of faeces for presence of eggs/larva of parasites. Submit faecal samples to veterinary diagnostic laboratory for confirmation.

Flat (Tape) worms

Except for few species that are seldom encountered, tape worms in general, are less harmful than round worms. *Diphylidium caninum* is the most common tapeworm of dog and virtually all stray dogs harbor this parasite. The infection is mostly insidious in adults with no apparent disease signs. The infected dog rubs the anus to ground or wall and passes cucumber seed or boiled rice like moving white worms in faeces, that disappear or stop movement after some time. This tape worm is not much harmful, but its complete removal is very difficult. It is transmitted through fleas and therefore, flea control is essential to stop the transmission.

It should be noted that many round and flatworms of dog can also infect man. They can cause serious health problems in children. Therefore, regular deworming and maintenance of hygiene is essential both for health of your pet and children.

Deworming

Deworming should be started at the age of 2 weeks and repeated after every 2 weeks until the dog is 3 months (12 weeks) old. Thereafter, deworm at monthly interval for next 3 months, i.e. up to 6 months of age. The dog more than 6 months old should be dewormed twice a year. It is advisable to use different dewormers alternatively. This gives better results and prevents development of drug resistance in parasites. Underdosing as well as overdosing, both should be avoided. Nursing bitches can transmit worms (Toxocara) to sucking puppies through milk. Therefore, pregnant bitches, should be given an additional deworming 3 weeks prior to whelping and for 3 consecutive days after whelping to get parasite free pups; even if, her normal deworming schedule is complete and updated.

The above described deworming schedule is standard but too rigorous to follow. An easy approach is to first deworm at the age of 30 days and thereafter every 6 weeks until 6 month of age. After 6 months, deworm after on interval of 6 months. This schedule is easy to follow, minimizes worm load to a safe level, but is not a standard full proof schedule.

Precautions

Deworming causes stress for few days. Therefore, it should be avoided in sick dogs showing signs of weakness, fever, loss of appetite, vomition or diarrhea, until necessary or recommended by a veterinarian. It is not advisable to go for deworming and vaccination on the same day. A gap of one week will rather give better results of both deworming as well as vaccination.

Deworming of sick and pregnant animals should be done only under veterinary supervision. Overdosing with dewormer can cause serious problem to pups or bitches. Dewormers available for human use should never be given without consulting a veterinarian. If any adverse symptoms, like reduced appetite, dullness and abdominal distension are observed after deworming, consult your veterinarian immediately. Always maintain a deworming record in a format given in the appendix.

❏❏❏

Chapter 11

Vaccination

Vaccination can protect the dog from many deadly diseases viz, rabies, parvovirus infection, canine distemper, hepatitis, leptospirosis, parainfluenza, kennel cough and corona virus infection. Therefore, proper and regular vaccination is essential to safeguard health of the pet. Different vaccines available for use in dog are described below.

1. Six/Seven in one

This a common name for many combined vaccines available in the market with different trade name (Canigen-DHPPiL; Megavac-6; Nobivac DHPPiL etc.). It can protect the dog from canine distemper, parvovirus, infectious canine hepatitis, parainfluenza and leptospirosis. Single vaccine consists of two vials, one vial contains freeze dried powder and other vial contains liquid. Liquid from one vial is to be withdrawn and poured in to the other vial containing dry powder. Both are mixed well and injected either subcutaneously (below skin) or intramuscularly (in the muscle). Remember, once the two vials are mixed, it should be injected within few hours; otherwise the vaccine may become ineffective. The schedule for administration is as follows:

1. *First dose* : 6-8 weeks of age
2. *Second dose* : 10-12 weeks of age
3. *Third dose* : after one year of the second dose.

Subsequent dosing, after one year of the last dose.

Recently, it has been observed that many dogs suffer from canine distemper or parvo virus infection despite vaccinated as per the above schedule. Therefore, an alternate schedule may be followed, in which combined canine parvovirus and canine distemper vaccine (Nobivac PUPPY DP *etc.*) is given, first at 6-8 weeks of the age. Then, second dose with "six/seven in one" is given at the age of 9-11 weeks. Third dose with "six/seven in one" is given at 12-14 weeks of age. In areas, where leptospirosis is common, separate vaccine for leptospira (Nobivac Lepto *etc.*) should be given; first dose at 9-11 weeks and second dose at 12-14 weeks of age.

2. Rabies vaccine

One ml of killed rabies vaccine (Nobivac Rabies, Raksharab, Rabigen *etc.*) is given, first dose at 12 weeks of age. Second dose is given at 16 weeks of age. This should be followed by annual booster vaccination. In case first rabies vaccine is given before 12 weeks of age, the same schedule should be followed, i.e. go for rabies vaccination again at 12th week and 16th week of age.

Post bite vaccination

If the dog is wounded during fighting with other dog, cat or monkey, go for post bite vaccination, preferably within 24 hours of the incident.

1. *If the culprit animal is not vaccinated for rabies:*

   Total seven doses of killed rabies virus vaccine should be given. Give 1 ml subcutaneous on day 0 (the day of first injection), 3, 7, 14, 28, 60 and on day 90.

2. *If the culprit animal is properly vaccinated for rabies:*

   Two doses of killed rabies virus vaccine should be given. First dose on day 0 and second dose on day 3rd.

A person having dog bite wound should always take post bite vaccination (with rabies vaccines for human use, like Rabipur etc.), even if the culprit dog is pet and properly vaccinated against rabies.

3. Corona virus vaccine

Inactivated coronavirus vaccine can be given, first dose at the age of 9 weeks and second dose (booster) at the age of 12 weeks. Adequate immunity is not achieved until 2-3 weeks after the booster vaccination. Thereafter, annual booster is recommended. Do not worry since the disease rarely causes death of the animal.

Vaccination of pregnant bitch

Vaccination in a pregnant or lactating bitch should be avoided. It may be harmful. If vaccination is due, shift it before pregnancy or after weaning (separation) of pups. Under special circumstances killed vaccines may be given to a pregnant or lactating bitch. It is a common belief that vaccinating a lactating bitch will provide protection to the nursing pups. But remember, at least one week is required after vaccination to activate bitch's immune system and antibodies to come in the milk. Also, the newborn pups can receive antibodies through milk only during their first 36 hours of the life.

Vaccination failure

Sometimes vaccine may fail and the vaccinated dog may develop the disease. Remember, no vaccine can give protection in 100% dog population receiving it. There are several reasons behind vaccination failure. Important among them are poor quality vaccine, improper administration, nutritional deficiencies in dog, sickness at the time of vaccination, interference by other vaccine administered after few days or by immunity (antibody) already present in the body and exposure of the disease prior to vaccination. At least one week is required for achieving immunity after vaccination. If the dog gets infection in between, disease symptoms may appear just after vaccination. In such cases, owner can wrongly jump to the conclusion that the sickness is due to administration of poor quality vaccine.

Points to remember

1. Pup before receiving first vaccination should not be allowed to mix with other dogs or bitches (except mother). Do not allow to go outdoors for long time.
2. Vaccine should be given only when animal is healthy. Check the rectal temperature before vaccination.
3. Always use a vaccine of a reputed pharmaceutical company. Check the date of manufacture, batch number and date of expiry.

4. Maintenance of cold chain during transportation and storage is very important. Any falut can make the vaccine ineffective. So always purchase vaccine from a reputed drug seller, who keeps the vaccine in refrigerator.
5. Vaccine should be stored at 4^0C (in chiller section). Do not place the vaccine in freezing section. Freezing denatures the vaccine.
6. Sticker over the vaccine vial should be removed and adhered to the vaccination record.
7. If more than one type of vaccine is to be given, give them on the same day, not after a gap of few days.
8. For a particular disease vaccine, a second dose after 2-4 weeks should be given, if the animal is being vaccinated for the first time to that disease.
9. After vaccination, observe the dog for half an hour. Occasionally, adverse drug reaction (hypersensitivity) may develop. If you observe any facial swelling, itching or restlessness symptoms, consult a veterinarian immediately.
10. A gap of two to three weeks between two different vaccines should be given to get better results.
11. Remember, no vaccine is full proof. A disease may develop despite proper vaccination.
12. Rabies is 100 % fatal disease. So do not take risk if you are bitten by any dog or in case of close contact of a dog (specially saliva) suspected for rabies. Consult a physician and take necessary action.

□□□

Chapter 12

Control of Ectoparasites

You must be aware about ectoparasites. They include mites, ticks, flea and louse. Mites are very small in size and not visible with naked eyes. They cause "mange" which has been described in Chapter 14. Ticks and mites are other important ectoparasites from pet health point of view. They suck blood and can transmit a number of infectious diseases. They also cause nuisance and may be responsible for training failure, since dog is unable to concentrate and is always busy in itching. In this chapter control of ticks and fleas are described in brief.

Tick control

Natural habitat of ticks includes dogs as well as environment surrounding the living area of the dog. For effective tick control, measures must be implemented for both the dog and the environment. Otherwise, ticks may reappear on the dog after a short time interval. Tick control in the environment also has two components, first is the removal or reducing space where ticks can hide, like bushes, tall grasses, old rugs, cracks and crevices in the floor, rodents and other animals. So try to keep the environment clean. Second aspect is to spray insecticides every month in the yard, kennel and living area of the dog. During winter season, i.e. November to February, tick population increases and hence treatment of the environment must be undertaken. Always use a comparatively less toxic, eco-friendly product and follow all the instructions written on label of the container. Insecticide powder should also be applied on the wall around the entire room, minimum up to one foot height above the level. Dog's beddings and other belongings must be treated simultaneously.

Tick control on dogs is the second component. Regularly check the dog for the presence of any tick. Products that can kill ticks (and other ectoparasites) come in different forms like sprays, dips, shampoos, collars and powders etc. All these are toxic for the dog as well, and hence proper care should be taken to avoid their exposure over eyes or accidental licking by the dog. Also, they are potentially hazardous for men, so take proper safety measures, like use of surgical gloves and masks while application. Different available products are as follows:

1. *Preparations requiring once-a-month application*: They are usually available as concentrated liquids and are applied on back of the dog. They contain permethrin, pyrethrin, imidacloprid, flumethrin (Tikkil power 1%; Flupor 1%) or fipronil (Spray Effipro 0.25%).
2. *Shampoos and soaps*: Medicated shampoos containing cypermethrin (Clinar pet 1%; Tikkil shampoo 1%; Cisaflux 1%; Furfree 1%) and carbaryl (Notix liquid 10%) are available in the market. Soaps containing cypermethrin (Clinar-M 1%; Cizabath 1%) and permethrin (Softas 1%) are also available. Apply over the entire body and leave for 5 to 10 minutes before rinsing. This will kill all the ectoparasites present over the body. Avoid application over eyes and inside ears. Some preparations have residual effects and are effective for long time after their application.
3. *Sprays*: Sprays containing insecticides come as aerosols or pump bottles. Spray over entire body, taking precautions to protect eyes and ears. It should be applied after bringing the dog in well ventilated areas like open ground or yard. Pemethrin (Spray Tic Tac 2%), pyrethrin *etc.* are available in spray form.
4. *Powders*: Powders containing pyrethrin, carbaryl (Notix talc 5%, Notix fort 10%) are effective against ticks as well as fleas. They

are applied over the entire body and allowed to act for 10-20 minutes. Then, take a clean cotton towel and wipe off extra powder present over the body. A bath after its application is not desired. They are usually safe for use in pups and small dogs.

5. *Dips*: Insecticides including amitraz (Ridd 12.5%, Taktic 5%, 12.5%; Ciza-Dip 12.5%) permethrin, pyrethrin, deltamethrin (Butox 12.5 mg/ml), fenvalerate (Ticomax 20%) cypermethrin (Dermeez 10%, Cutirose 10%, Pectocide 10%)etc. can be applied as dips and rinses. Desired dilution is made in clean water. Either apply over the entire body using a clean cotton cloth piece or dip the dog in a container containing insecticide solution. Before dipping, ear openings should be closed with cotton plugs. Take precautions to protect eyes and any wound, if present.

6. *Collars*: Collars containing insecticides (like flumethrin) are available for both tick and flea control. But they are effective when only few number of ticks are present. It is better to use them as preventive measure rather than for curative purposes. Different tick collars are available in the market (KILTIX; PREVENTIC etc.). Proper fitting and regular replacement of tick collar is essential, otherwise they may fail to act or can be dangerous to pet.

Flea control

Flea control is more difficult than tick control. This is because fleas can travel faster (they can jump a long distance rapidly) and survive for months without sucking blood. Adult flea remains on the animal most of the time, but other stages of their life cycle, including eggs, larvae and pupae are found in abundance in the environment, such as, in carpet, beddings, grass, furniture, rugs and corners of the room. Therefore, simultaneous adoption of flea control measures for dog as well as environment is essential. Different chemicals used for flea control can be divided into two groups, 1. adulticides, that kill the mature flea, and 2. Insect growth regulators/growth inhibitors that prevents an egg, larva or pupa to develop into an adult flea. Chemicals under second group are used for flea control in the environment, where only few adults, but thousands and lakhs of eggs are present.

Environmental flea control program should incorporate killing adult fleas and preventing immature stages to further development. Vaccum cleaning of carpets and floors (on weekly or monthly basis) are very effective and can remove up to 50 % of fleas and their developing stages. Spray of products containing adulticide plus insect growth regulator (IGR), like pyriproxyfen or methoprene are highly effective. They come in powder form, as spary or mist. Apply over the entire carpet or floor properly. Keep close watch on the environmental contamination and adverse effects on your family health. Special care is required, if someone in the family is asthmatic. Dog bedding and all belongings should also be washed and treated simultaneously. All places where dog roams inside the house should be cleaned. Fleas prefer to live in warm, moist and dark places where organic materials are abundant (debris, leaves, grass clippings, dust etc). Clean them first before applying any chemical. Fenvalerate is an excellent chemical for use as spray for environmental control. Outdoor spray may be repeated every 7 to 21 days, depending upon the product and gravity of the problem.

Flea control on pet is almost similar to that discussed in tick control on pet section. Anti-flea products are available as sprays, dips, powders, shampoos, collars and injectables. In addition, some oral drugs can also be given for flea control. Tablet Progam contains an insect development inhibitor and can be given once a month. It does not kill the adult fleas. So methods for killing adult fleas should also be applied simultaneously. Capastar tablet is a product that kills adult flea, but act only for 24 hours. So it can be given in conditions where quick relief is warranted. Ivermectin injection @ 0.2 mg/kg body weight, subcutaneously, is also effective against flea and tick problem, but action lasts only for one week. Flea combs are also available that have 32 teeth/ inch length. They can be useful when excess fleas are present on the body. Comb the dog patiently and dip all fleas collected in detergent water to kill. This is a useful method particularly for pups, pregnant bitches and dogs with poor body condition or wounds on skin, where use of chemicals for flea control is risky.

Preventive measures

1. Go for regular flea repellent spray (with or without insect growth regulators/development inhibitors) in living area of the dog and outdoor environment.

2. After return from other house, place, dog show or meeting with other dog and animal, give a flea bath before the dog enters inside the house.

3. Fleas usually have multiple animal host. They can suck blood from over 50 species of animals and can thrive even when no dog is available in the house. So control of wild rat, rabbit and cat population in surrounding area is essential.

❑❑❑

Chapter 13

Signs of Illness

Many times, we fail to appreciate that the dog is not feeling good or something is wrong from health point of view. In such cases, the disease advances and may require aggressive therapy. Early diagnosis and prompt therapy always help in early recovery. Since the dog can not tell about its problem, one has to rely only upon clinical signs and symptoms. Knowledge about various signs of illness is therefore essential.

Signs of illness

1. *Decreased appetite and thirst*: The food and water intake is either reduced or completely absent.
2. *Change in behaviour and temperament*: Dog may become more docile or aggressive.
3. *Decreased activity and alertness*: Dog may appear dull, prefers to remain aloof, hides in dark places and passes more time in sleeping.

4. *Abnormal activities*: Shivering, convulsions, circling movement, jaw champing, excessive scratching of a particular body part, excessive vocalization, barking or moaning.

5. *Abnormal discharges from natural orifices*: Loose motion, vomition, bloody discharges from nostrils, vagina, penis, gums etc., purulent thick discharges from eyes or nostrils and frequent urination.

6. *Abnormal locomotion*: Stiff gait, lameness, excessive vocalization when touched or coaxed to move.

7. *Abnormal respiration*: Increased respiratory rate, respiratory distress etc.

8. *Abnormal appearance*: Sunken eyes, emaciation, dry nostrils, swollen face, reddish or pale eyes, yellowish or reddish appearance of skin, foul smell coming from the body or mouth cavity, change in skin or coat colour, sunken or distended abdomen etc.

9. *Other signs*: Absence of urination or defecation, body appears either cool or hot, when touched.

Preparing a dog for visiting a veterinary clinic

1. Occasionally, the dog should be brought to a new house to meet new people or dog. Outdoor visit should not be only for medical purposes.

2. Train your dog at home to sit in relaxed position and allow handling and examination of different body parts like eyes, ears, mouth, feet and abdomen.

3. Praise or give a treat following good behaviour during examination and treatment.

4. Apply a neck collar and lead during visit to a veterinary hospital. Keep a muzzle of suitable size and a clinical thermometer (available for human use) with you.

5. Bring all records related to vaccination, old health problems and treatment given.

6. Give details of the disease history. Hiding any fact or observation can lead to wrong diagnosis and treatment.

Table 1 : Signs of illness related to different organ system dysfunction

Organ-system involved	Signs of illness
Digestive system	Vomition (frothy, yellowish, reddish, greenish), diarrhoea (blackish, reddish, yellowish), progressive weight loss, constipation, painful defecation, defecation following feeding, abdominal distension or discomfort after feeding
Respiratory system	Nasal discharges (watery, thick yellowish, reddish, foul smelling), coughing, snoring, difficult breathing, exercise intolerance
Urinary system	Reddish urine, not passing urine, difficult/ painful urination, dribbling of urine, frequent urination
Reproductive system	Genital discharges (vulva, penis; reddish, thick, bloody, foul smelling), mammary gland swelling, enlarged testicles, not coming in heat (breeding cycle), not conceiving after mating
Nervous system	Fits, loss of conciousness, partial or complete paralysis, changed behaviour
Skin problems	Itching, licking skin, reddish skin, scratches, pustules, scab formation, hair loss, foul smell from body/ hair coat
Eye problems	Discharges (watery, thick yellowish), blindness (complete/ incomplete), reddish/ cloudiness/ haziness/ ground glass/ blackish appearance of eyes
Ear problems	Frequent head shacking or ear scratching, head tilting, discharges from ear (thick, foul smelling), swelling of pinna, deafness (partial/ complete)
Bone, joint and muscle problem	Lameness, frequent head tilting, paralysis, pain on touch
Cardiovascular system (Heart and Blood)	Nasal bleeding, exercise intolerance, nocturnal coughing, non-productive (dry) coughing, weakness despite good health, faints while walking, open mouth breathing while walking

❑❑❑

Chapter 14 Infectious Diseases

There are many infectious diseases that can cause serious illness in dogs. Many of them are hazardous for human also because the disease can be transmitted to humans coming in contact of a diseased dog. Fortunately, most of them can be prevented by adapting proper hygiene and regular vaccination. Here, brief descriptions of only important infectious diseases are given.

Viral Diseases

Rabies

It is an incurable viral disease that can occur in man, domestic (cattle, buffalo, sheep, goat, horse *etc.*) and wild (monkey, mongoose, fox, bats *etc.*) animals. The virus is present in saliva of the diseased dog and transmitted to other dogs, man and animals mostly by deep bite. Symptoms of the disease may appear in few days (usually within 21 days) after dog bite. The disease in dogs occurs in two forms, furious form and dumb form. The furious form (also called as "mad form") is more common and is characterized by mania, restlessness, aimless wandering and biting at slight provocation. Later on, lower jaw paralyses, hangs and excess thick saliva drools out from the mouth. In dumb form, the dog remains calm and quiet, usually hides in the dark places like corners of the room and under bed and does not show signs of madness. In both forms, dog is unable to drink water despite thirst and does not recognize or disobey the owner. Later on, the hind quarters paralyze and animal dies. In case of bite to pet dog by stray or other pet dog, post bite vaccination should be given, even if, both the culprit and the sufferer are regularly vaccinated for rabies. If any dog is showing signs of the disease, isolate the dog and avoid contact with saliva. Rabies can be prevented by vaccination.

Canine Distemper

The disease is air borne and highly contagious, occuring mostly during the winter season. Pup in the age group of 3 to 6 months is at high risk. Anorexia, dullness, fever (103 to 105^{0}F), bloody diarrhea, vomition, nasal and ocular discharges and pustules on abdomen are important clinical signs of the disease. Immediate treatment is essential as the disease occurs mostly in the acute form. If the dog is young or weak, death may occur in untreated cases due to dehydration and septicemia. Properly treated dogs may recover within a week but fever may reappear after 10 to 15 days. Nervous signs like jerking movement of the hind legs and forehead muscles and champing of jaw may follow. The end result is either complete paralysis and death or recovery that can take few days to months. Since the disease is rapidly transmitted to other dogs, the sick animal should be kept in isolation. Vaccination, first at the age of 6 to 8 weeks and booster after one month is recommended. Adult dogs should be annually vaccinated. Vaccination may fail to protect the disease. Stray dogs are often source of infection and hence contact of pup and young dog with stray dogs should be avoided, particularly during winter months.

Parvovirus gastroenteritis

Canine parvovirus (CPV) infection is transmitted mainly by oral route (intake of infected food/ material) and causes high fever, vomition, bloody diarrhea with typical foul smell, dullness, dehydration and death. The disease is more severe in pups and weak young dogs. The affected dog initially may take water and vomit frequently. But later on, undergoes completely off fed and the temperature may return to normal or even subnormal. Similar symptoms may be observed in hookworm infection. If vomition is frequent no medication, water or food should be given orally for 24 hours. All medications should be given as injections during persistent vomition. The dog undergoing treatment may take one week or more for complete recovery. When vomition stops and the dog is ready to take food, small quantity of liquid or soft diet should be given initially. Since the virus is present in faeces and the disease is highly contagious, sanitary measures should be adopted to prevent its spread. For preventive purposes, pups should be vaccinated, first at the age of 6 to 8 weeks and second or booster dose after 4 weeks interval with killed monovalent or polyvalent vaccines. Pups born from infected bitch (which may not show any clinical signs or abnormality) or pups that are infected immediately after birth, may show signs of acute illness and die soon due to heart failure. Therefore, infected pregnant bitches should be vaccinated with monovalent vaccine one month before expected date of delivery.

Corona virus infection

It is primarily a disease of pups. Clinical disease caused by corona virus resembles parvovirus gastroenteritis. However, the disease is less dangerous than parvovirus infection. Symptoms include nausea, lack of appetite, vomiting and diarrhea. Coronavirus diarrhea typically lasts 2-4 days and very few puppies die.

Infectious Canine Hepatitis

It is a serious viral disease caused by canine adenovirus type I. Dogs of all age groups may be affected and severity of the disease varies from acute fatal form to mild or asymptomatic form. Infection occurs by oral intake of the infected material (virus). First clinical sign of the disease is fever, which may disappear within one or two days. But, few days after initial recovery, the second and more severe stage of the disease may appear. In this phase high fever, anorexia, abdominal pain (dog cries after pressing abdomen), vomition and diarrohea are common clinical signs. Later on, the eyes become hazy or opaque and the oral cavity may turn yellowish (jaundice). Reddish patches (due to subcutaneous hemorrhages) may appear over abdominal skin. Death may occur within 3 to 6 days after the second phase starts. In blood examination, decrease in number of white blood cells is commonly observed. No specific treatment is available. The disease can be prevented by regular vaccination.

Canine Parainfluenza Virus (CPiV) or Kennel Cough

CPiV is one of the main causes of the disease known as "kennel cough". Clinical symptoms include chronic coughing and nasal discharges, which are observed frequently during activity or excitement. Environmental factors, such as improper ventilation, cold and high humidity increase susceptibility to the disease. Secondary bacterial infections (mainly of *Bordetella bronchiseptica*) usually accompany enhancing severity of the disease. In uncomplicated cases, the dog may recover within 3 to 4 days. Cough syrups and antibiotics should be given, if respiratory signs are severe.

Bacterial diseases

Leptospirosis

It is a serious bacterial disease of dogs that can be transmitted to man. The bacteria can enter inside the body by penetrating the eye and oral mucous membrane. Few days after entry, bacteria multiply and may spread to the whole body through blood. It may damage all organs, especially liver and kidneys. High fever is observed, which may disappear after one week. In young dogs, the disease may appear in severe form causing high fever, nasal bleeding, bloody vomition and diarrhea. Jaundice may or may not appear. In less severe form, kidneys are damaged leading less urine production and difficulty in urination. Several laboratory tests are available for confirmatory diagnosis. The dogs affected with less severe form of the disease excrete bacteria in urine and act as a source of infection. High doses of antibiotics, like streptomycin and penicillin G or tetracycline should be given. Fluid therapy and other symptomatic therapy are also essential for early recovery.

Pyoderma

Pyoderma is bacterial infection of the skin resulting into pus formation. Symptoms include off smell, itching, pus and crust formation over skin. Since external skin barrier is poor in dogs, they are more susceptible for bacterial infections. Pyoderma also occurs secondary to mange. Maintenance of proper hygiene is essential. Regular bathing and grooming promote healthy skin and prevents pyoderma. Long term antibiotic therapy (for 10 days minimum) may be required. In case where only a small part of the skin in involved, application of antiseptic cream after removal of debris and washing of the infected area with cleansing soap may be helpful.

Parasitic Diseases

Blood parasites

There are several diseases in dogs caused by blood parasites. They are transmitted mainly by ticks (external blood sucking parasites). Tryapanosomiasis, Babesiosis, Ehrlichiasis and Hepatozoonosis are important diseases in dogs. The symptoms vary with the disease and may include fever, anemia, nasal bleeding, corneal opacity, weight loss, lameness, weakness and nervous signs. The diagnosis is based on microscopic examination of the blood. The animal responds well to the therapy, but relapses are common. Tick control is essential for prevention and complete cure.

Mange

Mange is a skin disease caused by mites (arthropode parasites). Mites are too small to be visible with naked eyes, but can be seen under microscope in skin scrapping of the diseased dog. *Sarcoptic scabiei* and *Demodex canis* are two important mange mites of dogs in India. Major symptoms of the disease caused by *S scabiei* (known as canine scabies) include intense itching, hair fall, reddish skin and scab/crust formation. Affected body parts mainly include abdomen, legs, chest and ears. The mites, sometimes (not always), cause disease in person coming in contact of the diseased dog. Itching is less intense in canine demodicosis caused by *D canis*, but, changes in skin like pustule/nodule formation, thickening, exudation and crust formation are more pronounced. The mild form of the disease is common in pups, but mostly cured without any medication. Treatment is required only if the pup is under weight or severely affected. The disease occurs more frequently during winter season, perhaps, due to compromise in immunity. Dog with good physical condition and on good nutrition recovers faster. Relapses of demodicosis are quite common; the disease may appear during winter and remain in dormant stage during rest of the year. The mite is supposed to be present in limited number even in healthy animals. The disease occurs only when they multiply rapidly in an uncontrolled manner.

Both types of mange are curable. Consult a vet. Continue the therapy for two more weeks after complete disappearance of symptoms. Incomplete treatment is the common cause to failure of therapy or relapses.

Prevention of infectious diseases

Maintenance of proper hygiene is essential for prevention of the disease. Dogs with good body condition usually have more power to fight against diseases. On the other hand, lean anemic and pot bellied dogs are more prone to infectious diseases. Regular deworming and vaccination should be followed. Proper care should be taken to avoid exposure to extremes of the weather. Give some extra multivitamin and mineral supplementation during winter season.

❑❑❑

Chapter 15 Non-Infectious Diseases and Problems

Excessive hair fall

A healthy dog should have a clean and shiny hair coat. Hair grows from hair follicle present in the skin, and after maturation, they becomes loose and fall. New hair emerges from the same hair follicle and in this way, replacement occurs. In dogs, 3-15 hairs emerge from one hair follicle making the hair coat dense. Hair coat of dog is broadly classified into normal, short and long depending upon the hair length and texture. Replacement of old hair with new one is a continuous process, which occurs in such a way that overall thickness of hair coat is maintained. However, the hair growth depends upon many factors including photoperiod, environmental temperature, hormonal status and nutrition. The dog shed hair coat twice a year, once during early winter then in early summer. During these days, owner may get annoyed or worried due to excessive hair fall. But, this is a normal feature and treatment is not required unless accompanied by other problems like itching, foul smell or complete loss of hairs in pathces. Excessive hair loss also occurs during pregnancy, lactation or several weeks after illness or mild fever. So check the rectal temperature regularly, if hairs are falling in excess. Other common causes of hair loss include hypothyroidism, allergy, skin infections, and prolonged administration of estrogen or corticosteroids. Supplementation of soybean oil (1 to 2 tea spoonful), cod liver oil capsules (1 to 2 capsules per day) and zinc (Syrup Nutricoat) can help in maintaining healthy and shiny hair coat. Bacterial infections of skin and hair follicles are commonly accompanied by foul smelling hair coat that appear ruffled due to itching and oozing of watery materials forming crusts. A course of antibiotics for one to two weeks can improve the condition.

Obesity

Obesity is a problem commonly observed in dogs in big cities, where they undergo minimal physical activity and exercise. The problem is more common in older one, specially after removal of testicles or ovary. Hypothyroidism may be one of the reasons of obesity. Moreover, junk foods (rich sources of calorie) are often served that contribute obesity to a great extent. In nut shell, obesity is the result of imbalance between calorie intake and calorie burn (exercise). Also, certain breeds like Labrador Retriever, Dash Hound and Pug are more prone. Boredom may also contribute to a certain extent, since dogs that are not having any business, keep on eating more and more. Obese dogs are often assumed to be well fed and healthy by obsessive owners. In a healthy dog, ribs can be easily felt behind skin and a moderate muscular layer. If the ribs are barely palpable and a thick, pliable, slippery mass is evident below the skin, the dog can be declared obese. On the other side, if ribs are palpable just behind the skin and depression between adjacent ribs is present, the body condition of the dog can be declared poor (dog may be suffering from ascites, chronic renal failure, parasitic burden etc). Obese dogs are lethargic and frequently suffer from joint diseases, lameness, liver disorders, heat intolerance, constipation, poor exercise tolerance and capricious appetite. Reproductive performance is also reduced to a certain extent.

Obese dogs should be fed diet with less calories, but high fiber and protein content. Total amount of food given per day should also be reduced, but reduction should be gradual since a hungry dog may start food begging and crying. It is also ethically deplorable. As a thumb rule, reduce the food less than 20 % of the normal diet of the dog. Alternatively, you can increase the bulk of the food without adding calories, like adding water to the milk and chokar to wheat flour (atta) used for making bread. But, at the same time, multivitamin, multi-mineral tablets, capsules or syrups should also be given at regular intervals to avoid deficiency diseases. Lean meat, chapatti, egg and fruits should be given. Potatoes, rice, sweets, fast foods, oily foods, cream etc. should be avoided. Increase in physical activity is must and the elderly dogs must go for outing regularly. Running and jumping for 30 minutes to one hour per day can help in prevention as well as cure of the problem. Efficacy of antiobesity drugs, used in human medicine is questionable. Provide some toys or company of other dogs, so that boredom can be avoided. Body weight of the dog should be regularly monitored and rapid loss should be avoided and considered alearning.

Motion sickness

Some dogs may be scared to travel by motor vehicles or air. They become nervous and may show anxiety, excess salivation, open mouth breathing, vomition and sometimes, diarrhea. Symptoms disappear when vehicle stops or voyage is over. Such dogs should not be given heavy food at least 10 to 12 hours prior to long journey. Use of antiemetics and sedatives are recommended. Consult any veterinarian and give prochlorperazine @ 0.12 mg/kg body weight (Tab Stemetil @1 tab/50 kg b.wt.) or metchlopromide @ 0.25 to 0.5 mg/kg body weight (Tab Perinorm @1 tab/10 kg b.wt.) one hour before the journey. A short break of 15 to 30 minutes after every 3 to 4 hours can also minimize the journey stress in the dog.

Chewing and eating inedible materials (Pica)

Pups and young dogs may develop habit of chewing and eating inedible substances like soil, grass, plaster, brick, bone, wood, cloth, shoe or some other household materials. This habit is a common feature in pups below one year of age, the time during which teeth and bone are growing and the dog is playful by nature. Provide some soft toys, like rubber balls and bone chews and give some calcium supplements. The complete cure is not possible, but this habit will decrease itself gradually with age. Check for the worm burden and deworm the dog regularly. Close confinement and boredom may also be a reason behind development of this bad habit. So make arrangements to avoid boredom. Sometimes the dog may show habit of eating own faces, which is known as "Coprophagia". This may be due to deficiency of some digestive enzymes, mild pancreatitis or pancreatic insufficiency or deficiency of vitamin B complex. In such cases, supplements containing vitamin B, amylase, pepsin etc. should be given regularly. Give plenty of fruits like papaya and pumpkin. Strict monitoring and punishment just after eating faeces are also essential. The dog should be removed from the place immediately after defecation. Firm "No" command can also help sometimes in trained dogs.

Aggressive behaviour

Growling, snapping, barking, lunging, and biting are different signs of canine aggression. Aggressive behaviour is often a problem; specially in certain breeds and those raised in a wrong manner. One should handle the situation patiently, keeping in view the normal dog psychology and behaviour pattern. Mishandling, negligence or wrong training may increase the problem. It's important to deal with these problems promptly.

There are different types of canine aggressive behaviour, depending upon the cause. Fear based aggression is the most common form. When a dog is anxious and feeling threatened, it may turn aggressive. It is a defensive action rather than aggressive behaviour. Biting or barking at strangers is mostly due to fear based aggression. Another example is growling of a dog, when someone stares at him or raises a hand or shows a stick. Fear aggression may be elicited even if the stranger or any situation is not really threatening the dog. Improper socialization is usually the cause of fear based aggression. The dog kept out door or in cages often become aggressive. Close contact with human beings and other dogs right from early days make a dog more docile. Territorial aggression is another form in which the dog becomes furious if other animal (mostly unknown dog) enters into his territory. In attempt to protect a man or an animal, the dog may also show aggressive behaviour (protective aggression). One specific type of protective aggression is maternal aggression, where bitch become protective of their puppies. In guarding or possessive aggression, a dog tries to protect the food, toys or any other belonging. Status related or social aggression is shown whenever a dog feels that its social hierarchy is disturbed. To avoid this situation, train your dog from early days that its position comes at the last in family hierarchy. A socially aggressive dog may growl if disturbed while resting or sleeping, or is asked to go away from the resting place. Redirected aggression may be shown when dogs are fighting and people try to separate them. Pain elicited aggression may be shown by a otherwise friendly dog, when touched or disturbed by any person or animal during pain.

Remember, aggression is a part of normal inherited behaviour of dogs. The difference between normal and abnormal lies only in threshold at which a dog displays aggressive behavior. Raising the threshold level makes a dog less likely to respond aggressively. This threshold can be raised using behavior modification techniques. How easily the threshold can be raised is governed by the dog's sex, breed, age, general temperament, selection and implementation of behaviour modification techniques.

Following points should be taken into consideration when any dog is showing aggressive behaviour:

1. Consult a veterinarian or dog psychologist or trainer, who will help you identifying the exact cause of aggression.
2. Spay or neuter your dog if showing social, territorial and protective aggression.
3. Avoid exposing to situations that elicit aggression. Keep the dog confined, and avoid unnecessary contact to safeguard yourself and the family.
4. Don't punish your dog for aggression; this is likely to have negative impact.
5. Handle an aggressive dog with patience. If the dog is possessive of food, treats or a certain place, don't allow him to access them. In an emergency, bribe him with something better than what he has. For example, if dog is possessive for a toy, offer him an egg as a reward for leaving the toy.
6. Never encourage or overlook the aggressive behaviour shown in excess.

❑❑❑

Chapter 16

Surgical Procedures

Tail docking

Tail docking is a kind of cosmetic surgery that is often done to meet the breed standard. It is performed only in Boxer, Doberman Pinscher, Miniature Pinscher, and certain other terrier and pointer breeds. The length of the tail to be preserved depends upon the breed, but generally one third of total length should be left after docking. The best time to perform is the first week after birth. At this stage, the tail docking induces less pain and stress. Always perform it when the pup is active, sucking milk and not showing any signs of illness. However, a pup may cry or show restlessness or pain signs up to few hours following the surgery. Maintenance of good hygiene and regular dressing is essential for early healing.

Ear cropping

In ear cropping, outer margins of the pinna (ear flap) is trimmed to give an attractive look. It is a kind of cosmetic surgery commonly performed in certain breeds of dog kept for show purposes. The procedure serves no benefit to the well being of the dog and is ethically deplorable. Ear cropping is generally performed in Great Dane, Boxer,

Boston Terrier and Doberman Pinscher. The operation is performed at about 8 to 12 weeks of age or soon after pup begins to lift the pinna. Cropping can also be done in adult dogs, but following operation, pinna may appear shoddy with uneven and coarse naked margins. When performed at early ages, it gives better results. Shape of cropped ear should be decided on the basis of breed and shape of the head in adult dog. Generally, for a long narrow head, longer ear looks more beautiful; while for a short, broad head, shorter ears are preferred.

Aural haematoma or blood blisters of pinna

It is common in dogs with a big and pendulous pinna. Internal bleeding due to frequent rubbing and scratching of the pinna is the main causative factor. The affected dog shows head shaking and repeated pawing at ears. Close examination reveals swelling of the pinna (ear flap), that appears egg like or round in shape and warm, soft, fluid-filled on touch. In long lasting cases, infection may set up, leading to pus formation. Therefore, consult a vet immediately, who will drain it surgically. The treatment of the disease causing excess itching sensation should also be treated, since haematoma tends to develop again even after successful surgery.

Birth control operation

Bitch

Birth control operation is the best way to avoid breeding. In females, the process is termed as spaying, ovariectomy (ovary removal) or ovario-hysterectomy (ovaries and uterus removal) and is carried out under general anesthesia. The best time to perform spaying is 3 to 5 months of age. Besides no risk of unwanted pregnancy, spaying has some other added advantages also. There is less risk to develop mammary tumor. Bleeding associated with heat cycle and chances of uterine infections are eliminated. Gathering of stray dogs around the house during breeding season stops. It is believed that spaying increases the life expectancy in a bitch.

Dog

Dogs can be neutered at the age of 7 to 9 months. Here both the testicles are removed under general anesthesia. The operation is simple than that of spaying since abdominal incision is not required. Neutering reduces male aggression and the dog becomes more docile. Roaming and mounting behavior during breeding season is also eliminated. Neutered dog does not show territorial marking by urine spray and usually starts urinating like a bitch. Risk of prostrate enlargement during old age reduces. Chances to develop hernia also decrease. But a neutered dog becomes more prone for obesity and hence diet should be adjusted accordingly.

Cherry eyes

Cherry eye is protrusion of the gland of the third eyelid (nictitating membrane). A reddish, soft, shiny mass is observed at the corner of eye, close towards nostrils (medial canthus). This actually occurs due to increase in size of the gland of third eye lid. It may be accompanied by irritation or frequent deposition of thick whitish secretions on eye corners. If the problem is mild, use of antibiotic and corticosteroids locally as eye drops or ointments may be effective, but relapses are common. Surgical removal of the gland is then only option left. However, after removal of the gland, the dog may develop dry eyes (keratoconjuctivitis sicca) since this gland provides lubrication to the eye.

Removal of fifth digit or dew claw

Like us, the dog have five digits. But only four are functional and the fifth digit (toe) is rudimentary. It is placed above the ground level and known as dew claw. In some dogs, dew claw may be absent from hind limbs at birth. But if present, it may grow excessively and cause self inflicted injury to eyes and ears. Therefore, it is better to remove the dew claw in hind limbs of the pup, preferably during first week of the life. At this stage, it can be easily removed with the help of scissors or surgical blade with less pain and bleeding. In adult dogs, general anesthesia and post surgical wound dressing are required.

Hernia (Umbilical hernia)

There are several types of hernia, based upon their location, nature of the content and size. Most of them require surgical correction and hence their detailed description is beyond the scope of this book. Only umbilical hernia will be discussed here. Umbilical hernia may be present at birth, but frequently observed at the age of 2 to 3 months, when a soft pliable mass (swelling) appears. Generally, it does not create any clinical sickness, but is often confused with developing wound or tumor. Differentiating features are absence of heat or pain when touched, location of the lesion and age of the dog. When the pup is placed in dorsal recumbency, *i.e.* abdomen and legs up and dorsum (back of the dog) touching the ground, hernia disappears. If the hernia is of small size (less than a 5 rupees coin in area), no surgical treatment is required. Just apply pressure bandage over the abdomen covering the hernia. It will decrease and disappear gradually. If the dog is showing signs of sickness, like abdominal pain or digestive disturbances or hernia persists after one year of age, consult the veterinarian.

❑❑❑

Chapter 17 Medication

Medication is required whenever a dog is sick. Medicines may be available in many dosage forms like injection, tablet, capsule, syrup, eye or ear drop, ointment etc. Use of different dosage form depend upon the disease, organs involved, severity of the disease, veterinarian's choice and owner's convenience. In this chapter, ways of administration of different dosage forms are described in brief.

Tablets, Capsules and Syrups

Administration of oral medicines may prove a difficult task for an owner, particularly when the dog is a fussy eater or the drug is bitter. One can hide the tablet inside any food material of dog's choice. It may include sweets, boiled egg, sausage, hollow treats etc. Tablets can also be given after crushing into fine powder and mixing with strong smelling substances like cheese, commercial semisolid dog food, milk, curd, lassi etc. Likewise, the drug present inside the capsule can be taken out by cutting the gelatin cap with razor blade and given to the dog after mixing with above edibles. Try to keep the quantity of food material small and offer it, when dog is hungry. Never mix the medicines with food in front of the dog, since they are intelligent animals and can conclude something is wrong with the food. Observe carefully after giving medicated food to ensure proper consumption. If the dog is gentle and co-operative, tablets and capsules can also be put directly into the throat. Make the dog to sit on a table with fore legs in extended position. One person should hold the animal and open the mouth gently, either with hand or with the help of two bandage pieces tied with upper and lower jaw separately. Neck is hold upright and tablet or capsule is dropped or popped deep into the throat. The mouth is closed and both jaws are hold together, so that tablet can not be expelled out. Gently strike or rub the throat or nose to facilitate swallowing. Praise the dog after process is over.

Liquid medicines like syrup or suspension can be given with the help of a dropper or plastic syringe. It is a time taking process and sometimes require patience. Allow the dog to sit with front legs in straight position. One person can control the dog with one hand and hold the mouth with upper and lower jaws together with other hand. The other person, with the help of thumb and forefinger separates upper and lower lip and makes a gap at the corner point (at oral commisure) and pushes the syringe or dropper filled with medicine gently inside on the dorsal surface of the tongue. When the syringe is in the middle of mouth cavity, release the medicine slowly and give some time to swallow. Gently rub or strike the throat, if required, to initiate swallowing. Some part of liquid medicine may dribble out during administration. Wipe out the mouth with clean towel or tissue paper after the process is over. Do not forget to praise the dog at the end.

Eye drops and ointments

One person restrains the dog in similar way as that for oral medication. Other person separates the eyelids with one hand and applies medicine with another hand. Nozzle of the dropper or tube should not touch the eye surface. Gently squeeze the required number of drops and allow the medicine to cover the entire eye surface. Hold the eye open for few seconds. Immediate closure of eyelids may result into drooling of liquid medicine through corners of the eye. Ointment is spread in a line along the side of lower eye-lid. Hold the eyes closed for some time, so that ointment liquefies and spreads over the entire eye surface.

Ear drops

Ear consists of three parts, external ear, middle ear and inner ear. External ear comprises pinna, the outer ear flap and ear canal, a tube like structure that extends up to middle ear. Ear canal is a L-shaped tube in dogs. Initially it runs downwards vertically and then turns sharply inwards. Therefore, simply pouring medicine at the opening of ear canal will not give an optimum result. Ideally, ear drops applied should reach up to the end of ear canal. Hold the pinna in outward direction before drug administration, so that the ear canal curvature is reduced and then release the drops. After process is over, gently massage the base of pinna from all sides to facilitate spreading of the drug. It is better, if the dog is restrained in the lateral recumbency with one ear touching the ground and the other ear ready for medication.

Ointment / Lotion/ Spray / Powder application over skin

Medicines for use over skin or wound surfaces are available in different forms like ointment, lotion, spray and powder. Individually, each of them is having certain advantages as well as limitations. They should be applied after cleaning the skin or wound surface with soap and/or water or as advised by veterinarian. Lotion is good for open wound, but requires repeated application. Ointment usually acts for long time but makes the skin or wound surface moist and greasy. Spray have better skin penetration and easy to apply, but most of them have an alcoholic base. Therefore, they may induce burning sensation when applied over open wounds or lacerated skin. Powder is a good option for eczema or moist wound with copious discharge. Antifungal deodorants and powders are also available in the market that can be tried, but have limited utility in dogs.

Injections

Administration of injectable drugs, by large, is the job of a pharmacist or a veterinarian. But, learning the technique of intramuscular or subcutaneous injection is easy and can solve the problem of frequent visit to a far situated veterinary hospital. Also, you can save the life of the dog in case of emergencies.

The ideal site for subcutaneous injection is loose skin over shoulder and head. Hold a fold of skin with the help of thumb and forefinger and insert the needle at the base. Ensure that the needle is placed in between the skin folds; it should neither come out from skin, nor cross the skin to enter into muscle mass. Then slowly inject the medicine. Intramuscular injections can be given in muscles of hind quarters, either on hamstring muscles or back side of hind quarters (semitendinosus and semimembranosus muscles). While inserting the needle, its direction should be away from the femur bone (caudally directed).

□□□

Chapter 18

First Aid and Emergency Management

Every owner should have preliminary knowledge about the first aid assistance and initial management during emergencies. A box containing necessary equipments, materials and life saving drugs should always be ready (Table 1). Check the box' contents regularly and replace expired drugs and other materials, periodically. Since oral medication, by large, are not applicable during emergencies, it will be of great help if someone in the family knows to give intramuscular or intravenous injections to a dog. Also, keep the telephone number of your nearest available veterinarian in your pocket diary or write it on the top of the first aid box.

Some drugs and equipments required during emergency conditions can also be procured and kept ready, specially if, one is having many dogs. On telephonic consultation and advice, one can inject necessary medications during life threatening conditions, before a veterinarian arrives. Sometimes, lack of emergency drugs and equipments may even paralyze the doctor during emergencies.

Table 1 : Materials and drugs to be kept in first aid and emergency aid box

First aid box: Scissors, Forceps, Clinical thermometer, Nail cutter, Ice packs, Syringes (2, 5 and 10 ml), Hypodermic needles (18, 20, 22 and 24 gauge), Cotton, Adhesive tapes (2 and 4", paper tapes or Johnson's tape), Bandages, Muzzle, Rubber gloves, Sprit, Betadine (Ointment and lotion), Paracetamole tablets (Tablet Crocin), Pressure bandage.
Emergency aid box: All the contents of first aid box plus Inj. Dexona, Avil, Adrenaline, Nikethamide, Atropin sulfate, Diazepam, Butrum-1 or 2, Diclofenac sodium, Sterysyl/ Stryptochrome/ Botropase, Normal saline solution (500 ml bottle), Drip set, Scalp vein/ Intravenous canula (18, 20, 22 and 24 gauge), Baby feeding tubes (5 and 6 no.), Endotracheal tubes, Ambu' bag, Laryngeoscope, Penlight

First Aid during Various Conditions

Bleeding wounds and cuts

Automobile accidents or some sharp objects may induce deep injuries leading to copious bleeding. First of all, apply cotton soaked with disinfectant solutions on that area and put light pressure for some time. Alternatively, if possible wrap the area with bandage to stop bleeding. If bleeding continues for few minutes despite all attempts, contact a veterinarian. If wound is lacerated or not so severe, clip the hairs around adjoining area and apply antiseptic solution like betadine or diluted dettol or savlon. Do not allow the dog to lick the area; either apply muzzle or neck collar. In case of old wounds, remove the dirt or necrosed tissues by gentle rubbing, so that the wound starts appearing fresh and pink and apply an antiseptic cream or solution. It is better to apply antibiotic powder than cream on the moist wounds. In case of copious bleeding from nose, restrict movement of the dog and apply icepacks or cold water over the forehead and muzzle. Contact immediately any vet, since it may have serious consequences.

Fracture

Fracture of limbs is commonly observed following jumping or some accidents. It is accompanied by signs of swelling, pain, abnormality of gait and posture. Fractured leg is generally held upwards and the dog avoids putting pressure on it or touching the ground during movement. In old cases, swelling is generally mild or may be even absent. The dog does not allow the affected part to be touched. Careful examination reveals cracking sound during movement and the limb can be displaced even in abnormal directions. If fracture wound is fresh and severe involving skin and muscles, wrap the wound with a clean cloth and try to stop bleeding by applying pressure. Rush to the nearest veterinarian. Do not attempt to align fractured bone as it may further induce injuries. While transporting the injured dog, keep the affected parts towards upper side not touching to the ground. You can keep a pillow or a fold of clean cloth underneath to provide support to the injured parts. If the injury is minor or no open wound is present, veterinary assistance can be delayed; by the time the dog should be chained or put in close confinement to restrict movements. However, unnecessary delay or negligence may result into prolonged recovery time or even permanent deformity.

Burns

Burn injuries may be caused by fire, steam inhalation, some chemicals or by chewing electrical wire. If burnt area is small, apply cold water or ice cubes continuously for 10 to 15 minutes. Do not rub burnt area vigorously. Apply Burnol or Silver sulfadiazine ointment gently. Do not allow the dog to lick the burnt part. Consult the vet immediately, if burnt area is large or animal appears restless.

Poisoning

Poisoning with pesticides, paints, batteries, rat bait etc. may be encountered particularly if a dog is in a habit of chewing all objects. Common symptoms include vomition, diarrhea, severe weakness, recumbency, high or sometimes low rectal temperature, convulsion, frothy discharge from mouth and loss of consciousness. If you observe the dog ingesting poisonous substances, immediately induce vomition by pouring concentrated common salt solution on the back of tongue. But never try to induce vomition in a recumbent, comatose or an overexcited dog. It is better to go for immediate veterinary help. Record the details about the poison and inform the doctor about your doubts or observations. Raw egg white acts as good absorbent for different poisons and can be given in any dog suspected for recent poisoning.

Vomition

If a dog eats too much or ingest some indigestible or putrefied food, vomition may occur once or twice. Sometimes, the dog feels abdominal discomfort, runs here and there, eats some grasses and vomits to get a relief. This is a normal phenomenon. But, when it continues for long time, treatment is required. The presence of parasites or indigestible materials or some mild but chronic infections in digestive tract are common reasons. Frequent vomition during a short time span always warrants immediate attention and treatment. Vomitus turns yellowish or greenish thick and oily, when stomach is empty. If any delay in treatment is expected, give tab perinorm @1 tab/10 kg b.wt.; Tab Stemetil @ 1 tab/ 50 kg b.wt. Injectable drugs, like inj Perinorm @ 1ml/10 kg b.wt.; Inj stemetil (if vomition is severe)@ 0.5 ml/40 kg b.wt. are better since tablets may fail to act due to vomition soon after their administration. Only soft liquid diet, like water with added glucose and Electral powder, curd diluted with water (Lassi), rice gruel, vegetable soups etc can be given, if the dog is able to digest or vomition is not too frequent. But, if the dog vomits soon after taking water or liquid diet, stop giving anything. Immediately rush to a veterinarian, who will give intravenous fluid as per the requirement.

Diarrhoea

Diarrhoea is a common problem encountered in pups and young dogs. Some pups may not digest milk and hence shifting on milk free diet may solve the problem. In such pups, curd may be given. Excess feeding or calcium supplements (syrups) may also cause loose motion. Foul smelling, coffee coloured/blackish loose stool associated with vomition, once or twice a day may be due to worms in the stomach. Red or dark brown colour faeces suggest presence of blood in stool. Consult the doctor and submit faeces (5 to 10 ml or gram) in a clean bottle for examination.

If vomition and diarrhea occur simultaneously, rush immediately for vet help since severe water loss may be dangerours to the life. Mostly, it is related to some viral infections like parvo-virus, canine distemper and corona virus. Tell the veterinarian about deworing and vaccination status, details of food served during recent past, ingestion of inediables, poison etc. You can give tab Dependal M@ 1 t.s.f./10 kg b.wt. or syrup Powergyl @1 t.s.f./10 kg. b.wt. twice to thrice daily, if diarrhea is mild and delayed treatment is expected.

Allergy or wasp bite

Sometimes dog may show symptoms like facial swelling that develops quickly (within few minutes) and restlessness just after giving some medicine, vaccination or just after arrival from outdoor visit. This may be due to allergy. Wasp bite results into swelling around bite site. In both conditions, you can give tablet Avil 25 mg @1 tab/25 kg b.wt. or tablet Cetirizine 10 mg @ 1 tab/20 kg b.wt.

Dog bite/ fight

This commonly occurs during breeding season when several males are competing for a female in heat. Stray dogs may also attack a pet during outdoor visit. Bite wounds should be cleaned thoroughly with alkaline soap (Washing soap); and betadine or some other diluted antiseptics, like savlon or dettol should be applied. Hairs present around wound site should be removed with the help of scissors. Bandages or adhesive tapes should not be applied unless necessary and the wound should never be sutured. Visit the nearby vet and ask for the post bite vaccination (See vaccination chapter). Following a severe fight, the dog may not take food or water, remain dull and depressed for few days due to pain and mental shock. Your attention and love is needed during these days.

Heat stroke/ Hyperthermia

The dog is considered as a non-sweating animal, since the skin does not have functional sweat glands except over nose and in between foot pads. Excess body heat in dogs is lost mainly by panting and salivation. The capacity to loose excess body heat is limited in dogs and this makes them more prone for heat stroke. Conditions that induce excess heat production or impair heat loss, like vigorous exercise, running, excitement, excessive barking, dehydration, less water intake, hot and humid climate, close confinement during transportation and closure of mouth (that stops panting) are common causes of heat stroke. Sudden rise in the body temperature above critical level occurs over a short period of time and it may reach above 104^0F. The dog fallen victim of heat stroke shows signs of recumbency (unable to get up), rapid panting and open mouth breathing, increased heart beat, restlessness and reddish eyes (congestion). Such dogs should be left calm and quite and should not be disturbed or forced to get up or walk. Pour plenty of chilled water over the body and keep under electrical fan. Ice cubes can also be put over the head region. If the animal is thirsty, give chilled water or ice for licking. Injection Novalgin or Fevastin (Paracetamole) @ 1ml/10 kg. b.wt. can be given intramuscularly.

Fits or Seizures

Fits are quite common in some breeds. The affected dog lies down and shows sudden jerky movements of all body parts, jaw champing, frothy salivation and unconsciousness. After few minutes, consciousness returns, but the dog may remain dull and depressed for the whole day. Some dogs show signs of mental excitement following recovery from fits. It is not a fatal disease unless accompanied by some accidents during fits or some other generalized disease. Complete cure is difficult, but the disease responds well to therapy. Leave the dog undisturbed, where it has fallen and started showing fits. Only protect from external hazards and self-inflicted injuries. Limbs and body may become stiff for some time, but will be relaxed automatically. If possible, try to keep the head in high position by putting a pillow beneath the head. Dog may go off fed for few hours, but appetite and thirst are resumed soon. Do not disturb much for 1 to 2 hours after recovery. It may be very much embarrassing for you to see your dear pet suffering from frequent episodes of fits. But do not panic. Consult a vet, if fits are frequent. A thumb rule is that the medication is not required if fits are coming once a month or even less frequently. But, if fits are more frequent, go for medication.

Difficulty in Whelping (giving birth)

Difficulty in whelping is seldom observed in bitches. If a bitch fails to give birth even after 4 hours parturition pain, go for veterinary assistance. Veterinary consultancy is also essential, if a full term pregnant bitch is off fed for more than a day, showing signs of pain intermittently, but not giving birth or the bitch is appearing dull, depressed and lethargic for a long time. Check the rectal temperature twice daily, prolonged low rectal temperature is alarming. If a bitch is off fed, dull and rectal temperature is sub normal for more than 48 hours, consult a vet immediately. Greenish discharge coming from genitalia before whelping is also an alarming condition. Bitch with large litter size may get exhausted during whelping. You can offer hot coffee or tea during whelping.

□□□

Chapter 19

Communicable Diseases

There is a long list of diseases that can be transmitted from the dog to human beings (Table 1). Such diseases are called as zoonotic diseases. Children, ladies, old and sick persons and those living in close contact or involved in feeding and daily care of the dog are more prone. Here only important zoonotic diseases are discussed in brief. For detailed information, readers are advised to visit the official website of WHO and OIE.

Rabies is the most important zoonotic disease that can spread by dog bite, contact of infected saliva through abraded skin, wounds or eyes. Do not allow the pet to lick your body part, if it does, wash the area properly with some alkaline soap. Remember, rabies virus is present in saliva of the dog even 10 days before onset of the symptoms of the disease. Never take risk, even if, you have minor bite by your regularly vaccinated pet dog. Rabies is a 100 per cent fatal disease; that means if the disease occurs in man, no treatment or cure is possible and death is the ultimate outcome. Always consult a physician and take post bite vaccination. If cost of vaccination is a constraint, take at least half of the scheduled doses. Danger is more in deep bites and bite in highly innervated areas (in areas where pain sensation is more, like finger tips, face *etc.*). Never cover or suture the bite wound unless suggested by a doctor.

Parasitic zoonoses are another important group of diseases that frequently occur, but mostly remain undiagnosed. *Balantidium coli*, *Entamoeba histolytica* and *Giardia* spp cause enteric infections, diarrhoea and abdominal cramp, vomition and other related signs. They are transmitted mainly by contaminated food or water. Many times the disease is mild and is cured by antidiarrhoeal drugs. *Toxoplasma gondii* is another important protozoa that can seriously harm a pregnant lady by causing abortion or abnormalities in newborn child. Therefore, gardening in area where dogs and cats play or defecate should be avoided. There are many round and tape worms, that can cause serious health hazards specially in children. Eggs or larvae of *Toxocara canis* and *Ancylostoma caninum* (hook worm) can cause creeping skin eruptions or visceral larva migraines, while *Echinococcus granulosus* (Tape worm) larvae may form cysts in brain. *Diphylidium caninum* (Tape worm) occur commonly in dogs and can infect human infants (itching in anus region).

Leptospira spp can be transmitted by skin penetration or ingestion of water contaminated with dog urine. It causes multi-organ failure in man. *Brucella canis* infection may cause undulant fever, infertility and sterility in adult human beings. Dogs can also transmit tuberculosis and streptococcal sore throat in man. There are many fungal diseases that can be transmitted from dog, causing ringworm or other systemic infections. Scabies in dogs can also be transmitted to man.

Regular deworming and vaccination of pet dogs are essential to minimize chances of spread of zoonotic diseases. Housing area of dog should be regularly cleaned and disinfected and excreta (urine and faeces) should be disposed taking all hygienic measures and precautions. Avoid close contact of pet specially with children, pregnant women and old members of the family. Never allow sharing bed and utensils. Sick dogs should be kept isolated and treated promptly. Wear protective gloves, shoes and spectacles while handling sick dogs. After attending sick dogs, wash hands and feet thoroughly with soap. Never allow licking the dog your body parts. Pets should not be allowed to go in close contact with wild animals and stray dogs. A healthy dog should be active, playful with smooth and glossy hair coat, free from skin diseases, bad odour or parasites. Meat or fish should never be served uncooked, since they may contain parasitic cysts or larva.

Table 1 : List of important zoonotic diseases

Disease	Major complications/ signs
Bacterial diseases	
Brucellosis	Abortion; chronic mild fever and headache; reproductive problems
Leptospirosis	Septicemia, kidney damage, multiorgan failure
Tuberculosis	Coughing, chronic wasting
Septic sore throat	Painful throat, fever
Viral diseases	
Rabies	Hydrophobia, mania
Mumps	Swelling behind lower jaw
Parasitic diseases	
Amoebiasis	Dysentery, dehydration
Giardiasis	Diarrhoea, dysentery
Balantidiasis	Diarrhoea
Toxoplasmosis	Abortion
Ascariasis	Round worm disease, pneumonia
Hydatid diseases	Brain cysts
Larva migrans	Skin eruptions, itching, organ failure
Hook worms or whip worms	Skin disease
Dracunculosis/ Guinea worm disease	Skin eruptions
Flea tape worm disease in child	Anal pruritus
Scabies	Skin disease, itching, eruptions
Flea allergy dermatitis	Skin disease, itching, eruptions
Fungal diseases	
Ringworm	Itching, thickening of skin
Candidiasis	Skin disease

❑❑❑

Chapter 20

Breeding Management

Breeding is an important aspect of dog husbandry. A good breeder manages to get optimum breeding performance and can earn handsome money by selling pups. Knowledge about the basics of dog breeding is essential for every dog owner.

Breeding system

Pedigree (history) of both dog (sire) and bitch (dam) should be examined before planning the breeding program. However, it should not be the sole criteria, since good phenotypic characters according to breed standards of both sire and dam are also crucial for getting good quality pups. Depending upon ancestors of sire and dam, breeding system can be classified into three classes, inbreeding, line-breeding and cross breeding.

1. Breeding between close relatives, like brother and sister, sire and daughter, dam and son come under inbreeding. Here, phenotypic and genotypic characters of pups resemble very much to their parents. In other words, there are more chances that all pups will grow to resemble their parents. But, such pups are more

prone for congenital and genetic defects and generally have poor disease resistance capacity. This breeding system is more popular among breeders, since there are more chances of getting pups like their parents.

2. The second system is called as line breeding, in which distant relatives of a family, like cousin brother and sister, half-brother and half-sister, grand daughter and grand father, grand mother and grand son are allowed to mate. This system also gives good results if phenotypically good sires and dams are bred.
3. Out breeding is the third system, in which sire and dam belong to different families. This is the least practiced breeding system now a day, since phenotypic characters of pups are unpredictable.

Both dog and bitch become sexually active at an age of 6 to 12 months. Large breed dogs may take more time, upto 9 to 12 months or even 2 years. Bitches of small breeds usually come in first heat at an age of 6 to 9 months. Most bitches come in heat (estrus) twice a year, once in the month of August to September and the next in the month of March to April. Some large breed bitches may come in heat only once a year. Breeding cycle in a bitch can be divided into 4 stages, i.e. proestrus, estrus, dioestrus and anoestrus. Proestrus lasts for 2 to 15 days (average 9 days) and is characterized by swelling of vulva with presence of some mucoid discharges initially. Later on, thin reddish discharges (bleeding) come that may continue for one week. This stage is followed by oestrus stage, which lasts for 1 to 15 days (average 9 days). This is the only stage when the bitch is receptive to male and allows mating. The third stage is dioestrus that lasts for 60 to 90 days. Vulval swelling is reduced and discharges gradually disappear. The last stage is anoestrus, which is the period of sexual rest. It may vary from 2 to 10 months duration till the next cycle starts.

Always escape the first heat and allow mating in second estrus cycle. This provides an opportunity to mature genital organs completely before conception. As a thumb rule, do not allow a bitch or a dog for mating before one year of age. Male dogs should not be allowed more than 3 mating a week. The ideal time for mating a bitch is in between 9 to 14 days from the day bleeding started. Three matings on every alternate day, starting from day 9 post bleeding, is the best practice to follow. Young bitches may be nervous at first mating and may not allow mounting to an unknown partner. Therefore, arrange meetings of dog and bitch 2 to 3 times before the breeding season starts, so that they can develop friendship or at least become familiar to each other. It is better to take the bitch to the dog rather than taking a dog to bitch house. Mating should be arranged in a calm and quiet place.

Mating usually last for 30 to 40 minutes. At the end, after dismounting, dog's penis "locks" inside the vagina and both partners stand close to each other laying hind quarters in opposition. It takes another 30 minutes to end the 'locking' naturally. This facilitates sperm transportation and fertilization. Allow them to stand quietly and wait till locking ends naturally. Any attempt to separate them forcefully may result into injury to genital organs and failure to conceive.

Table 1 : Breeding record of a bitch

S.No.	Date of first bleeding	Date of mating			Date of whelping		Number of puppies	Remarks
		First	Second	Third	Expected date	Actual date		

❑❑❑

Chapter 21

Care of Pregnant Bitch

Pregnancy diagnosis

Pregnancy diagnosis can be done manually in a lean relaxed bitch by abdominal palpation in between day 28 to 35 post mating. But this is neither an easy nor an accurate method. Ultrasonography and radiography are two valuable diagnostic tools that can be used, both for pregnancy diagnosis as well as monitoring foetal status. With real time ultrasonography, pregnancy diagnosis can be done as early as on day 25 post mating. Ultrasound can also help in differential diagnosis of uterine enlargement that may be due to normal pregnancy, pyometra, foetal mummification or some other uterine abnormalities. Radiography can also serve the purpose, but have certain limitations. Here pregnancy diagnosis is based upon observation and counting of foetal skeletons which can be first radiographed only after 45 to 55 days of mating. Number of foetus can be easily estimated by counting number of skull/axial skeleton visible in radiograph. Presence of gas in the uterus and collapse of the calvarium or axial skeleton suggest foetal death. Foetal heart rate can be counted by real time ultrasonography and a rate less than 100 beats per minute indicates foetal distress, which may result into foetal death, abortion or foetal mummification.

Stages of pregnancy

Normal pregnancy can be divided into 3 stages, 1. pregastrulation stage (day 0 to 12 post mating), 2. embryonic stage (day 13 to 30 post mating) and 3. fetal stage (day 31 till whelping). Embryonic stage is the most crucial since embryo is highly sensitive and vulnerable to different stressors, drugs and teratogenic agents. During embryonic period (i.e. day 13 to 30 post mating), deworming and vaccination specially with strong dewormers and live vaccines should be avoided. Different drugs like carbaryl, diazenon, dichlorvos, griseofulvin, cortisteroids (dexamethasone, betamethasone etc.), phenobarbitones, primidone and tetracyclines should not be given to bitch since they can cause foetal deformities. The other two stages of pregnancy are thought to be less prone to harmful effects of these drugs. However, it is better not to use them during entire pregnancy period. Hormonal therapy with progesterone, testosterone etc. should never be undertaken except under veterinary supervision.

The pregnant bitch should be shifted to a clean, quite area of the house, about one week prior to expected whelping date. Some bedding in the form of folded blanket and clean old newspapers should be provided. Balanced nutrition is crucial for health of pregnant bitch as well as proper foetal growth and development. A housing system or shelter like wooden boxes, child's wading pool or bathing tub can be provided, which will help preventing pups from going away from mother and will protect them from adverse climatic conditions. An artificial source of light and heat like electric bulb hanging above 3 feet from the box is recommended during winters. Hairs present around mammary glands and vulva should be trimmed and the area should be wiped with some mild antiseptic solution daily, during last week of pregnancy.

Delivery of pups (Parturition or Whelping)

Recording rectal temperature twice daily during last week of pregnancy is advisable. Usually rectal temperature falls abruptly to reach 97 to 98°F before 24 hours of normal parturition. However, this temperature fall is transient and reaches again to the normal range before parturition starts. Average gestation period in dogs is 62 ± 2 days. Whelping occurs normally between day 58 to 78 post mating. There are 3 stages of whelping. In stage I, that last from 6 to 12 hours, the bitch becomes restless and may show open mouth breathing and nesting behavior. Similar signs may be shown several times during the last week of pregnancy; hence it is difficult to identify this stage. In stage II, cervix dilates, uterine contractions start and the bitch try to deliver pups by contracting abdominal muscles (straining starts). Appearance of foetal membranes or foetus from vulva, abdominal contractions or straining shown by bitch are signs of stage II labor, which may last until delivery of all pups. Generally, a bitch delivers all pups in 2 to 4 hours after onset of stage II labor, but it may take up to 12 hours. Bitch may relax and take some time between deliveries of two consequent pups. In stage III, placenta is delivered. This follows after delivery of every one to two puppies. Bitch may try to eat placenta. Therefore, remove the placenta away, soon after release. Eating one or two placenta may not be harmful, but excess intake may cause digestive upsets. Bitch get exhausted and hence relax and take some time to deliver the next puppy. Hot beverages, like coffee or tea may be offered during delivery to provide some energy.

If the bitch fails to deliver pups despite completion of full term pregnancy or several hours after dilatation of cervix and appearance of foetal membranes, or there is doubt that some puppies are not delivered even after 12 hours of the first delivery, rush for veterinary assistance. Any abnormal signs like rise in rectal temperature, trembling, weakness, depression, frequent licking of water, and prolonged restlessness also warrant medical interventions, specially if the bitch is underweight or going to whelp for the first time. Care should be taken if only single puppy is detected by ultrasonography or radiography or the bitch suffered abortion, pyometra or dystocia during previous pregnancies.

Soon after birth (within 1 to 3 minutes) clean the nostrils and mouth cavity of the pup with the help of dry cotton or a towel. Remove placenta, fluid meconium or any debris if present. If excess fluid is present, hold the puppy gently and slowly swing downwards several times. If respiration does not start itself, rub the chest and face with dry towel and gently press and release the chest 2 to 3 times in 4 to 6 seconds. One or two drops of doxapram or diluted adrenaline can be put on the tongue of pup. Every possible care should be taken to protect newborn puppies from cold exposure. A temperature range of 28 to 30°C is suitable for newborn pups. Allow them to suck (breast feeding) after whelping is complete and mother is ready to attend the newborns.

❑❑❑

Chapter 22 Aging

Each passing day brings certain changes in mental status, behaviour pattern and physical activities of a dog. Like human beings, life of a dog can be divided into different phases; growth, maturity and aging.

Early growth and maturity

A pup matures mentally as well as physically faster than a human baby. A dog matures in about $1/15^{th}$ of the average lifespan, while a human child matures in about $1/5^{th}$ of the average lifespan. A small breed dog matures faster and lives longer than a large breed dog.

The middle age

Middle phase of the life, roughly from 2 to 6 years of age, can be called as "Golden Years" or "Healthy Years". During this phase, dogs mostly remain healthy, active and productive. However, some may fall sick frequently even during golden years, while others may enjoy health and vigour even beyond this phase. There are several factors that govern health status and healthy years of a dog.

a. *Breed*: Some breeds of dog are more prone for certain diseases. Pure bred dogs are generally more susceptible for different diseases than cross bred or mongrel dogs.

b. *Genetic make up and diversity*: Close inbreeding (breeding with closely related partner) increases disease susceptibility while out breeding (breeding partners from different blood lines) increases disease resistance. There are many diseases that are genetically inherited and individuals suffering from them should not be used for breeding.

c. *Diet*: Availability of balanced diet according to age, breed, physical activity *etc.* is essential for maintenance of health.

d. *Housing, management and assigned work*: Each dog breed has been developed for specific purpose. Housing, other management conditions and work assigned to dogs should match accordingly. If a Rottweiller, for example, is kept as a companion dog and not given proper exercise and living space, may fall sick. On the other hand, if a companion breed is used as a working dog and given too much exercise, arthritis and other musculoskeletal diseases can develop. Therefore, it is better to select a breed according to the purpose and availability of resources and infrastructure.

e. *Other factors*: Proper deworming, preventive vaccination and health care also contribute to health status. Spaying and neutering decreases the cancer risks and are supposed to increase healthy years of a dog life.

The old age

Signs of aging start to appear after 6 to 8 years of life. Age related changes in dogs, by far, are similar to those observed in human beings. There is loss of tooth; hearing and vision are compromized. Hair coat often becomes thin and skin becomes dark due to diffused hair loss and increased pigmentation, respectively. Coat color may change in certain breeds like Neapolian Mastiff. Nails become loose and discoloured. Senile dogs become less active and prefer to remain calm and quiet most of the time. Their calorie need decreases by 30 to 40% and hence become more prone to obesity, if the diet is not adjusted accordingly. The senile dogs frequently suffer from arthritis, gastrointestinal upsets, kidney problems, cataract, skin infections, dental problems, halitosis, prostrate enlargement and mammary tumors. Heart diseases, though less common in dogs, can occur during old age.

Dog years versus human years

For describing growth and development at any particular age, "dog years" are often compared with "human years". The actual years of a dog's life is called as "dog years" while "human years" is the equivalent age of a human being. There are several formulas and tables available for converting dog years into equivalent human years. Roughly, one dog year may be taken equivalent to 7 human years. But this thumb rule fits better in only medium to large sized breed only after 3 years of age. Other methods for calculation are given in table 1 and 2. Several internet sites also provide facility for direct conversion of dog years to equivalent human years.

Life expectancy of different breeds

Life expectancy varies with breed. In general, it is more for smaller breed and less for larger breed. Table 3 gives approximate life expectancy of common dog breeds.

Table 1 : Dog years equivalent to human years: method one

Dog years	Human years
I	15 years
IInd Year	15+7 = 22 years
IIIrd Year	15+7+7 = 29 years
Subsequent years	Add 4.5 for each subsequent year

Table 2 : Dog years equivalent to human years: method two

Dog years	Human years			
	Average body weight of an adult dog			
	2-10 Kg	10-20 Kg	20-40 Kg	> 40 Kg
1	15	15	14	12
2	23	24	22	20
3	28	29	29	28
Subsequent year	Add 4 (for each year)	Add 4.5 (for each year)	Add 5 (for each year)	Add 7 (for each year)

Table 3 : Life expectancy of common dog breeds

Life expectancy	Breed
6 to 8 years	Bulldog, Bullmastiff, Great Dane,
9 to 11 years	Doberman Pinscher, Rottweiler, Boxer, German Shepherd, Bull Terrier, English Cocker Spaniel, Irish Setter, Samoyed, Old English Sheepdog
12 years or more	Beagle, Chihuahua, Chow Chow, Dalmatian, Greyhound, Pekingese, Mongrel, Afghan Hound, Golden Retriever, Pomeranian, Boxer, Poodle, Tibetan Terrier

❑❑❑

Chapter 23 Care during Old Age

Better availability of health care facilities and increased owner awareness have resulted into marked increase in average life span of pet dogs during recent years. Like human beings, dogs also undergo some age related changes that make them more prone to certain diseases or problems (Table 1). Most of these changes are irreversible, but proper care can delay their onset. Old dogs require regular health check up, preventive medication and dietary modifications. To safeguard the health during old age, following points should be kept in mind.

1. *Regular check-up*: It can help in early identification of health risks. Annual vaccination program provides an opportunity to perform a full physical examination and would be an ideal time to recommend further screening. Health check-up should be carried out more frequently in dogs with history of serious illness. Record of vaccination, deworming, prior illness and treatment given, all should be presented to the veterinarian. All aspects and doubts should be discussed without hiding any fact. Examination of hair coat (infection, hair loss), nails, abdomen (pain, distension, swelling, fluid), oral cavity, tooth (foul smell, tartar, gum

infection), ears (wax, infection, foul smell), eyes (cataract, dry eyes) and prostrate gland in male should be done thoroughly. Certain laboratory tests may be needed for evaluation of functional status of vital organs. They include complete blood count, urine analysis, estimation of random blood glucose level, SGPT (ALT), SGOT (AST), AKP, Plasma/serum creatinine and blood urea level. Other diagnostic tools like ECG, ultrasonography and radiography can also be performed. Hypothyroidism is a common problem in geriatric dogs. Therefore, any history of lethargy, diffused hair loss, heat seeking behavior and obesity must be followed by thyroid function tests.

2. *Deworming and Vaccination*: In old dogs, capacity to fight against infectious diseases decrease. Therefore, deworming and vaccination should be done regularly.

3. *Dietary modifications*: In mature dogs, the energy requirement decreases with advancing age. Therefore, reduce the calorie intake, otherwise the dog may become obese. Obesity further increases risk of cardiovascular, respiratory, hepatic and musculoskeletal problems. Carbohydrate rich diet is only recommended in patients with kidney or liver problems. High quality protein sources that can be easily digested, should be provided. They include egg, liver and other animal sources. Cereal proteins are not utilized as efficiently as animal proteins. High protein diet should be avoided in renal and hepatic diseases. Home made foods, like boiled vegetables with little spice and salt with bread or boiled rice can be given in such dogs. Giving small quantity of food at frequent interval is better than large quantity given once or twice daily. Seasonal fruits add palatability besides serving a rich source of vitamins and other nutrients, hence should be given on regular basis. Chocolates, biscuits, snacks and other fast food items should be avoided. Fat is rich in calorie and should not be given in excess. Its intake should be carefully controlled in the presence of liver diseases, pancreatic diseases, hyperthyroidism and other causes of hyperlipidaemia. If appetite is reduced or dog is only taking small quantity of food (during sickness), fat may be increased in the diet. As long as the food contains sufficient quantities of gluconeogenic amino acids and fat, there is no extra dietary need of carbohydrates. Fibers (insoluble carbohydrates) may be beneficial in prevention of constipation and maintenance of normal gastrointestinal

function. High fiber diet should be avoided in chronic diarrhea and mal-absorption syndrome. Water-soluble vitamins are lost from the body in the urine. In case of increased urine production their dietary supplementation should also be increased to compensate the loss. Vitamin intake should also be increased in dogs with impaired hepatic functions.

4. *Exercise*: Limited but regular exercise is helpful for maintenance of normal health in old dogs. But vigorous exercise should always be avoided.

5. *Hygiene*: Daily grooming is essential for maintenance of healthy hair coat. Dog should be bathed with medicated dog soap or shampoo, once weekly. Presence of fleas, ticks and louse should be immediately taken care of, because they spread a number of infectious diseases beside causing irritation and sucking blood.

6. *Oral health*: Dental tartar is a common problem in geriatric dogs. Negligence of oral hygiene may exacerbate the condition. Bacteria grow rampantly, attack tooth and gum and may result in painful tooth or gum, premature tooth loss and halitosis. Secondary respiratory tract infection is uncommon but serious sequelae. The dog should be presented periodically to a veterinarian for examination of oral cavity and removal of dental tartar.

Table 1 : Common health problems and underlying cause in geriatric dogs

Common Diseases	Clinical signs and symptoms
Anemia	Reluctant to move or run, depression, gums appear whitish (less pink than normal)
Cancer	Abnormal persistent swelling or wound, that fails to respond the treatment, weight loss, reduced appetite, weakness etc.
Dental disease	Difficulty in eating, reduced appetite, foul smell from mouth, excess salivation, bleeding gums
Diabetes	Weight loss, increased thirst and urination, urine appears thick, whitish, leave stain over floor after cleaning and drying and attracts ants
Eye problems/ Cataracts	Eyes appearing dry, thick discharges depositing at corners, cloudy appearance, bumping into objects
Heart disease	Weakness, coughing especially at night, fainting, reluctant to move

contd...

Hypothyroidism	Hair loss, thin skin, lethargy, heat seeking behaviour and weight loss
Joint disease	Difficulty in rising after rest, reluctant to move or jump, dullness, lameness
Kidney disease	Vomition, loss of appetite, weight loss, weakness, oral ulcers, black tarry stool, painful abdomen
Liver disease	Reduced appetite, vomition, yellow gums and eyes, weakness
Obesity	Overweight, difficulty in getting up, reluctant to move, fluffy appearance
Prostate enlargement	Urine dribbling, difficulty in defecation, pain
Urinary stones	Difficult urination, blood in urine, urinary incontinence

□□□

Chapter 24

Traveling with a Dog

If you are going on a tour during holidays, stay of the pet dogs becomes a big problem. They can be shifted into house of any relative or friend. Boarding hostels for dogs are also available in big cities. But, sometimes, no option is left and you may have to include your dog in the team. Some dogs cope up journey stress very well, they rather enjoy the journey. Some dogs, however, may cause trouble. There are some important points to be taken into consideration while traveling with a dog.

Traveling by car

1. Inside the car, the dog should be restrained using pet seat belt or keeping the dog in a transportation box/crate. The box should be secured well within the car, so that it is fixed well to its position. Ensure proper ventilation inside the car.
2. Do not allow the dog to keep the head out of the window. Otherwise, the dog may be exposed to excessive dust, fumes or some harmful substances.
3. Only light food should be given before the journey. If dog has taken heavy meal, postpone the journey for 3 to 4 hours.

4. Keep some favorite food of the dog to offer during the journey breaks. Feeding and watering bowel must be kept in the luggage.
5. During warm weather, use air conditioning system. Go for journey breaks every 2 to 3 hourly. Offer cold water/cold drinks in between.
6. Never leave the dog in a closed car. Suffocation/heat stroke may be fatal.
7. If the dog is showing symptoms of heat stroke, viz., excessive open mouth breathing, weakness, red eyes and gum, high temperature and fast pulse, place the dog immediately in an open area and pour plenty of cold water on the head. Keep a wet towel over the body, and if possible, keep the dog under eclectic fan. Consult the nearest available veterinarian.
8. During journey break, allow the dog to walk in open for few minutes. But, do not leave the dog to run loose. Always secure the dog with collar and lead; otherwise, the dog may run away, fight with other dogs or meet any automobile accident.
9. If there is a history of motion sickness, take the preventive measures. Go for frequent journey breaks (every 1-2 hourly).

Traveling by train

Booking as luggage

1. Dog can be booked and carried in the luggage/brake van. Specially designed dog cages are usually available in brake van. Contact the parcel office for booking the dog.
2. Large dogs which cannot be carried in the dog-box of a brake van will be carried in a special vehicle at the same rate and condition as for horses.
3. Charges of booking will vary with the type of train and weight of the dog. They will be charged at Scale 'L' (luggage rates). Minimum charge, Rs. 10/-per dog. Brake Van (Dog-Box)- charges will be increased, if weight exceeds 30 kg.

Booking for travel with owner

1. A passenger can take pet dog along with him in AC First Class or First Class only, provided he/she reserves either a two berth or a four berth compartment exclusively for his/her use, paying the due charges.

2. Dogs are not allowed to be carried in AC three tier coach, AC chair car coach, sleeper class and second class coach.
3. Charges of booking will vary with the type of train and weight of the dog. They will be charged at Scale 'L' (luggage rates). Minimum charge, Rs. 10/-per dog. Charges will be increased if weight exceeds 60 kg.
4. Dog kept as "Seeing Eye" by any blind person can be transported in AC first class or first class compartment after paying charges equivalent to that for carrying a dog in brake van. The dog must bear collar and chain.
5. Fellow passengers in the compartment should not have any objection for transportation of the dog in the compartment.
6. If fellow passengers subsequently object to the dog remaining in the compartment, the dog will be shifted to the Guard's van, without refund.
7. A lady traveling alone with children under 12 years of age in a first class compartment may take one dog with her in the compartment on payment of charges at the Dog Box Rates, subject to a minimum of Rs. 10/- provided that, if another lady enters the compartment, the dog can only be allowed to remain in the compartment with her consent.

Fine for unbooked dogs

1. A passenger carrying a dog unbooked will be charged as per the rules.
2. If a dog is kept in reserved compartment, charges will be six times the Luggage Scale Rate subjected to a minimum of Rs.50/- .
3. For placing the dog in dog-box, one will be charged at double the dog-box rate for the distance between origin of the train to the point of detection and at the box-rate for the distance left. But, minimum charges will be Rs. 20/- for each dog.

Note

1. *All charges are to be paid in advance.*
2. *Owner will have to make their own arrangements for food and water for the dog during the journey. He/she will also be responsible for disposal of faeces and urine in a hygienic way.*
3. *Dog health certificate and vaccination record may be asked to produce at the time of booking.*

Traveling by air

A dog can travel by air in domestic flights, either in passenger section or in the cargo hold. Indian Airlines, Jet Airways and Jet Lite provide facility for traveling of dog in cargo hold. Before loading a dog in cargo section, the pilot of the plane should be informed in advance, so that temperature of that section is adjusted accordingly.

1. The dog should be properly dewormed and vaccinated. Carry the deworming and vaccination record during the journey.
2. Procure a health certificate from a registered qualified vet mentioning that the dog is physically fit for air traveling.
3. Procure an IATA specified dog cage of suitable size. Dog is to be kept in the cage during the journey. Attach a sticker on the crate bearing name of the dog, name of the owner, flight information, destination and arrival contact name and number. A big arrow should also be there to indicate which side of the cage is to be kept upward.
4. Some airways have fixed maximum size of the cage that can be transported in to the plane. For example, Jet Airways do not allow a cage bigger than 53″ X 48″ X 34″.
5. Keep some dry food like biscuits and some absorbent bedding materials to be used during journey.
6. Dog and cage should be checked in 3 hours prior to the flight time. Offer water to the dog before entering the airport. For queries related to dog travel, contact the cargo department.
7. Before boarding into an aircraft, remain in the boarding area to confirm that the dog has been loaded.
8. After boarding, confirm boarding of your dog. Ask to the flight attendant, or if necessary, from the captain.
9. During long layover, you can claim your pet and take it for a walk.
10. After reaching destination, claim the dog as early as possible.
11. Before changing plane, claim and recheck your dog.

□□□

Chapter 25

Import of a Dog

Dogs are imported under the provision of Livestock Importation Act, 1898, known as Act no. 9 of 1898. This act has been amended several times since its inception and some other acts have also been passed to regulate issues related to import of livestock and pets. Quarantine and certification facilities were started in India during fourth five years plan (1969-79). Import stations were approved which include Mumbai, Chennai, Kolkota and Cochin sea ports; Mumbai, Chennai, Kolkata, Cochin, Delhi and Tiruchirapalli air ports; Attari (India-Pakistan border) railway and bus stations. Initially quarantine period for dogs and cats were fixed as 40 days. However, it can be expended up to 90 days as per the Model Rules 1961. But, now it is usually left over discretion of the quarantine officer posted at the import station. Quarantine facilities, at present, are only available at New Delhi and Chennai air ports. The veterinary officer posted at import/ quarantine stations perform detailed clinical and laboratory examinations to ensure that the dog is healthy and free from any disease. The officer can recommend for quarantine in case of sickness or suspicion of any disease. Unvaccinated dogs and cats originating from countries, where rabies exists should be vaccinated on arrival and can be quarantined for a period up to 30 to 40 days. During this period, the entire cost of maintenance, feeding and other expenses has to be paid by the importer. Unvaccinated dogs and cats originating from countries free from rabies and not exposed to rabies infection, should be vaccinated on arrival and kept under restraint by the importer for one month.

If the dog is suspected to suffer from any infectious disease not reported in India or some other potentially dangerous disease, it may be seized and euthanized without the consent of the importer. Livestock Importation (Amendment) Act 1953 also empowers state government to make rules for the detention, inspection, disinfection or destruction of imported livestock and pets and their accessories.

A purebred good pedigree dog can be imported from various countries across the world. Pups with good pedigree records from a country native for a given breed, can be purchased at lower cost. Pups in the age group of 8 weeks to 6 months are ideal for import. Import of the dog soon after purchase is not recommended; wait for some days so that the dog adjusts well with the person accompanying during journey. Import of dogs, up to two per passenger may be allowed at a time, subjected to the production of the health certificate from the country of origin and examination of the said pets by the concerned quarantine officer. In such cases, the passengers may not be asked to produce the import licenses or import sanitary permits. A copy of standard health protocol while bringing dog is given at end of this chapter (See Customs Circular no. 94/2002 dated 23.12.2002 regarding Import of pets under baggage).

Steps in non-commercial import of dog as excess luggage via air to India

a. *Following are essential requirements (at export station) for import of a dog to India:*

   1. *Microchip implantation record*: Dog should have a microchip (with ISO Standard 11784 or 11785) implanted for identification purpose. No other identification method is acceptable. Scanner for the microchip should also be kept with the dog crate.

   2. *Rabies vaccination certificate*: Dog must be vaccinated (with killed rabies vaccine) for rabies. Rabies vaccination certificate must bear the microchip number implanted in the dog.

3. *Health certificate (Form 7001):* Health certificate issued within 10 days of the flight by any USDA accredited veterinarian should be procured in the country of export. The certificate should state that the dog has no clinical signs of aujosky's disease, canine distemper, rabies, leishmaniasis, leptospirosis and tuberculosis.

4. For import from USA, all the above three certificates should be send to the local USDA for their stamp of approval before boarding in plane at export station.

b. All domestic and international airlines allow travel of any dog in only International Air Transport Association (IATA) specified cages. Such cages are made up of fiber and available in different sizes to accommodate dog of different sizes. *The IATA specifications for cages are as follows:*

1. The cage must be made of a sturdy plastic and large enough for the animal(s) to stand, turn around, and lie down. All four sides of the cage should have ventilation. It should fit under the seat in front of you and should have a waterproof bottom.

2. The cage must have a all around secured locking system with the pins extending beyond the horizontal extrusions above and below the door.

3. Water and food bowls must be attached to the inside of the front door and be refillable from the outside without opening the door.

4. Live animal stickers should be pasted on the top and sides in letters at least one inch tall.

5. If wheels are attached with the cage, they should be removed or taped securely during the journey.

6. The container must be identified with the pet's name and owner's contact information.

c. Pet dogs should accompany their owner (or any authorized person) during the travel.

d. Airlines usually allow one pet per passenger and a maximum of two pets per cabin. Airlines flying large aircrafts also accept dog for transport in cargo.

e. After arrival in India, get no objection certificate (NOC) from quarantine officer posted at animal quarantine station.

f. Paste a duplicate copy of NOC over the crate/cage of dog.

g. Original copy of the NOC has to be produced to get the pet dog released from the custom officer at the Airport in India.

h. Go to Animal Quarantine Station, where quarantine officer after clinical examination of the dog, issues a temporary Health Certificate. Dog may have to stay at animal quarantine station for 30 days.

i. After a lapse of 30 days, obtain a health certificate from a local veterinarian. This is to be produced at the animal quarantine station. Then the quarantine officer will issue a permanent health certificate and you can bring the dog home.

Annexure-I

Animal Health Certificate for Import of Dog into India

I. OWNER

Name and address...

II DESCRIPTION

Species of animal......................................

Age or date of birth....................................

Sex...............................

Breed.............................

Colour............................

Coat type & marking/distinguishing mark.................................

Identification number..

III. ADDITIONAL INFORMATION

Country of origin..

Countries visited over the past years as declared by the owner (give dates) ....

IV. DESTINATION OF ANIMALS

Country of destination ....

Name and address of consignee ....

V. SANITARY INFORMATION

The undersigned Official Veterinarian certifies that the animal/s described above and examined on this day:

a) shows no clinical sign of diseases including rabies, canine distemper, parvo virus infection, leptospirosis etc..

b) has been vaccinated for rabies (in case it is more than three months of age) within the time limit recommended by the manufacturer of vaccine licensed and approved by the exporting country (name of the vaccine, batch number and the date of vaccination must be shown on the veterinary certificate)

Official stamp

Issued at .... on ....

Name and address of Veterinarian ....

Signature: ....

F.No.495/27/2001-Cus.VI; Government of India; Department of Revenue; Ministry of Finance & Company affairs; (Central Board of Excise & Customs)

❑❑❑

Chapter 26

Kannel Clubs and Registration

The Kennel Club of India (KCI, Head office: Chennai) is the apex professional body, that manages dog registration, kennel club registration, accreditation of dog breeders, organization and monitoring of dog shows throughout India. It is affiliated to The Kennel Club (London, UK) and is associated with Federation Cynologique International (FCI) and Asian Kennel Union (AKU). The KCI is an ISO 9001-2000 certified organization. Indian Kennel Gazette is a monthly magazine published by The KCI. There are more than 45 KCI registered regional Kennel Clubs in India (Table 1).

KCI is also responsible for maintenance of breed standards. The KCI registration is must for participation in KCI dog shows. The registration certificate carries records of 5 generations of the pup. At the time of whelping, a KCI representative visits the breeder to ensure parentage of pups and the breed characteristics of parents. Prefix "Ch" is used for the parent, declared champion in any KCI dog show. The cost of a pup/dog increases with the number of "Ch" appearing in the KCI registration certificate.

Procedure for KCI Registration

For getting any certificate or transaction with KCI, annual subscription of KCI monthly magazine, Indian Kennel Gazette (IKG) is essential. If the certificate is to be delivered via registered post, one will have to pay Rs 30/- extra. The postal address of KCI is as follows

Kennel Club of India

No. 28 (89) AA block, First Street

Anna Nagar

Chennai- 600 040

Tamil Nadu, India

E mail: kennelclub@eth.net; kenclub@md3.vsnl.net.in

a. When parents are already registered to KCI

1. Registering the litter

For registering a litter, parents should be KCI registered dogs. Fill up the form "A" and litter registration form, get them signed by appropriate persons at suitable places. Fee for litter registration per puppy (60-120 days) is Rs. 300/-, which can be paid in the form of a demand draft, in favour of the 'Kennel Club of India', payable at Chennai. Forms and demand draft can be dispatched via mail or courier. The litter registration form must reach KCI within 4 months of the date of birth, failing which, the pups will be registered in an unknown pedigree parents group.

b. When parents are not registered to KCI

1. Registering dog with unknown pedigree parents

Fill up Single Dog and Declaration form. Get your dog certified by any nearest available KCI authorized person or judge (Table 2). The KCI judge will issue a certificate in a prescribed format. Send the declaration form, certificate issued, 3 coloured photographs of the dog signed by the KCI judge on their back side with a demand draft of Rs 150, in favour of the 'Kennel Club of India', payable at Chennai. The KCI registers the dog as "Registration with Unknown Pedigree".

2. Registering an imported dog

Following documents are required to register an imported dog, when the dog is received as cargo:

1. A copy of the airway bill as proof of importation.
2. A KCI single dog application form duly filled.
3. A xerox copy of the receipt for money paid to the airport authority as clearing charges on the arrival of the dog.
4. A xerox copy of the health certificate and the quarantine officer's certificate at the port of clearing.
5. A xerox copy of the custom duty receipt, if paid.
6. The export pedigree in original along with its xerox copy.
7. If the pedigree is in language other than English, then it should be accompanied by a translation of the Pedigree by an authorized representative of the consul of the country, from where the dog is imported.
8. The dog should be micro-chipped and DNA tested for identification.

Transfer of ownership

Fill up the transfer of ownership form and get necessary signatures at appropriate places. Send the duly filled form along with original KCI registration certificate. Fee for transfer of ownership is Rs 100/- per dog. KCI will issue a new registration certificate.

Change of name

Fill up the change of name form, suggesting three different names. Attach the original KCI registration certificate. If the dog is registered with the breeder's Prefix/Affix (Kennel name), the name of the dog cannot be changed. If you have a kennel name registered with the KCI, the same can be added along with the existing registered name provided the number of letters does not exceed more than twenty four. The fee for this purpose is Rs.250/-, that can be send in the form of a demand draft, in favour of the 'Kennel Club of India', payable at Chennai.

Following forms can be downloaded from KCI Chennai website (http://www.thekci.org/downloadpage.aspx)

1. Litter A and B
2. Single dog
3. Prefix and affix
4. Change of name

5. Declaration
6. IKG subscription form
7. Transfer of ownership
8. Entry
9. IKG Ad contract form

Breeder's Accreditation Scheme

The KCI has started breeder's accreditation scheme, aiming to encourage breeding of only healthy dogs free from genetically transmitted disorders, to follow basic good practice of breeding, to safeguard owner's interest and welfare and to prevent frauds in sale of pups. Entry fee for the scheme is Rs 1000/- and it is to be renewed every year after furnishing the necessary requirements and depositing Rs 1000/- as annual renewal fee. Under this scheme, breeder has to commit certain agreements with KCI. The KCI authorities then visit the kennel to ensure that the kennel fulfills all necessary requirements for this scheme. The details about the scheme can be downloaded from the KCI website.

Table 1 : KCI registered Kennel Clubs

Delhi Kennel Club
Mr. Rajiv Shandilya(Hon.Sec)
3500, Kuchalalman, Delhi Gate
Delhi -110006
Ph: 91-(0)11-3260345

North of India Kennel Club
Dr. Samar Mahendran (Hon. Sec)
1, Krishi Vihar Shopping cmplx
Opp. Panchsheel Enclave
Josip Broz Tito Marg
New Delhi -110048
Ph: 91-(0)11-6217419

Capital City Canine Club
Mr. S. Madhok (Hon.Sec)
KD -25 Pitampura
New Delhi -110034
PH /Fax:91-(0)11-7251316

Noida Kennel Club
Mr R. Shankar Rao, (Hon.Sec)
1472, Arun Vihar,
Sector 37, **Noida** -201303
Ph: 91-(0)11-8-574780
Fax: 91-(0)11-8-552323

Kanpur Kennel Club
Mr. R.M. Dutta (Hon. Sec)
111A/160, Ashok Nagar,
Kanpur -208012
Fax: 91-(0)512-544766

Oudh Kennel Club
Mr. K.K. Trivedi (Hon. Sec)
C-784, Sector C, Maha Nagar,
Lucknow U.P -226004
Ph: 91-(0)522-75691

Rohil Khand Kennel Club
Dr. Abhijit Pawde (Hon Sec)
C-45, Kurmanchal Nagar Extn
P.O. Bihar Man Nagala,
Izatnagar **Bareilly,** U.P. -243122
Ph: 91-(0)581- 448409
Fax: 91-(0)581- 444965

Uttar Pradesh Kennel Club
Mr. V.K. Joshi (Hon. Sec)
No 2, Improvement Trust Flat,
Havelock Road, **Lucknow** -266001 - UP
Ph: 91-(0)522-229412

Taj Kennel Club
Mr. S.P. Malik (Hon Sec)
Malik Ville,
9, Tagore Nagar, Heera Bagh,
Agra - 282005 Ph: 91-(0)562-570789

Doon Valley Kennel Club
Mr.Sachindra Singh(Hon.Sec)
19/1, Subhash Road,
Dehradun -248001
Ph: 91-(0)135-651086

Amritsar Kennel Club
Mr Yogesh Tuteja (Hon.Sec)
71, Dayanand Nagar, III, Lawrence Road,
Amritsar; Ph: 91-(0)183-222612

Kohinoor Kennel Club
Dr. S.S. Bhatti (Hon.Sec.),14, Model Town, **Jalandhar City**

Ludhiana Kennel Club
Dr. B.S. Gill (Hon. Sec)
322-C, Bhai Randhir Singh Nagar
Ludhiana -1 Ph: 91-(0)161-457447

Patiala Kennel Club
Mr. G.P. Singh Brar (Hon. Sec)
14 B, Hira Nagar,
Patiala - 147001

Chandigarh Kennel Club
Maj. Trilochan Singh(Hon.Sec)
1156, Sector 33/C,
Chandigarh Ph: 91-(0)-172-601437

Tristar Kennel Club
Mr. Amit C.S. Negi (Hon. Sec)
87, Maharana Pratap Marg,
Ambala Cantt -133001
Ph: 91-(0)171-22677

Bihar Kennel Club
Mr. B.K.Sinha (Hon. Sec.)
Asst. Gen. Manager(Personnel)
TISCO; 4-1-C, Road,
Kaiser Bungalow,
Jamshedpur -831001
Off::Ph: 91-(0)657-423507
Res: Ph:91-(0)657-230887

Orissa Kennel Club
Dr. S.K.Ray (Hon.Sec.)
M -109, Baramunda Housing Board Colony,
Bhubaneshwar -7510033
Ph: 91-(0)674-555633

Calcutta Kennel Club
Mr. Tilak Prasad Ray (President)
5, Alipori Park Road,
Calcutta -700027
Ph: 91-(0)33-2477825

North Calcutta Kennel Club
Mr. Chandrasekhar Sarkar (Hon. Sec.)
54/4 Kali Charan Sett lane,
Calcutta -700030
Ph: 91-(0)33-5576362

Calicut Kennel Club
Mr. Rolad Jude Godfrey (Hon.Sec)
Akbar Travels of India
Kashkhand Chambers,
Bank Road, **Calicut** -673001
Ph: 91-(0)495-56802

Malabhar Canine Club
Mr. Arangil Girish Kumar (Hon. Sec)
17/811, Reghupuram,
Puthiyara, **Calicut** -4
Off Ph: 91-(0)495-722783
Res Ph: 91-(0)495-722733

Calcutta Canine Club
Mr. S.J. Mandal and Mr. S.S.Chatterjee (Hon.Jt.Secs.), P 123,CIT Road,
Scheme No: 52,
Entally, **Calcutta** - 700014

Burnpur Kennel Club
Mr. Bidyut Baran Patra (Hon.Sec)
G-3/1, road no: 16,
P.O.Chhotodighari Dist.**Burdwan, West Bengal** - 713326 Ph:91-(0)342-230790

New Bhopal Kennel Club
Mr. Arvind Dubey (Hon. Sec.)
17, Kalpana House,
Mandir Mahavir Road,
Bhopal - 462001
Ph: 91-(0)755-748127

Palghat Kennel Club
Mr. Jayan Menon (Hon. Sec)
c/o Instumentation Ltd.
Kanjikode West (P.O)
Palakkad -678623
Off Ph: 91-(0)491-566127

Madras Canine Club
Mr. C.V. Sudarsan (Hon. Sec)
51, 7th Cross Street
Shenoy Nagar
Chennai -600030
Ph: 91-(0)44-6260693

South of India Kennel Club
Mr. S.J. Lajapathie (Hon.Sec)
Oak End, Ootacamund
Nilgiris - Tamilnadu
Ph: 91-(0)423-42443

Kodaikanal Kennel Club
Mr. Rajagopal (Hon Sec)
"Nutshell" - Convent Road,
Kodaikanal, Tamilnadu

Hyderabad Canine Club
Mr. Kiran Chitnis (Hon.Sec)
Chitnis House
6-3-347/10/Dwarakapuri Clny,
Panjagutta,
Hyderabad - 500082
Ph: 91-(0)40- 593461

Andhra Pradesh Kennel Club
Mr. R.K. Bakshi (Hon.Sec.)
A/2, Vallabhdass Building,
Public Garden Road,
Nampally, **Hyderabad** -500001
Ph: 91-(0)40-3204500.
APKC Website: http://www.apkc.org

Bangalore Canine Club
Ms. Rajalakshmi Balasubramaniam (Hon.Sec.)
108-W, Trinity Woods,
Sarjapur Road,
Ambalapur Village,
Bangalore -560034
Ph: 91-(0)80-5720177

Mysore Kennel Club
Dr. B.C. Ramakrishna (Pres)
630, 17A, Main Road,
6th Block, Koramangala
Bangalore -560005
Ph: 91-(0)80-5532636

Mumbai Kennel Club
Mr Uday Kulkarni (Hon.Sec)
19B, Santhal Bldg, ONGC Complex,
Bandra Reclamation,
Mumbai -400050
Ph: 91-(0)22-6431710
Fax: 91-(0)22-6410544

Bombay Presidency
Kennel Club
Ms. Sheila Naharwar (Hon.Sec)
9, Garden Homes, 1st Road, Khar(W)
Bombay -400052
Ph: 91-(0)22-6000146

GSD Club of India
Mr. Sanjay Desai (Hon.Sec)
c/o Atur Chambers, 3rd Floor
2 A, Moledina Road,
Pune -411001 Ph: 91-(0)20-631105
Fax: 91-(0)20-631110

Poona Kennel Club
Mr. Sanjay Desai
B -6, Hermes Park Society (R)
Bund Garden Road,
Pune -400001
Ph: 91-(0)20-626823

Gujarat Kennel Club
Mr. Ashok Krishnadas(Pres)
ZG, Premises,
Munjmahuda Padra Road
Baroda -390020

Thrissur Kennel Club
Mr. Sushil K. Maratt (Hon. Sec)
General Medical Associates
Cooper Building
Thrissur – 680001; Kerala

Trivandrum Kennel Club
Mr. A. Prathab (Hon. Sec)
Meera Mahal, Thycaud,
Trivandrum - 14
Ph: 91-(0)471-327040

Cochin Kennel Club
Mr. Bejoy Varghese(Hon.Sec)
PKV, Transports& Agencies
Congress House Junction
M.G Road,
Kochi -11 Ph: 91-(0)484-347873

Coimbatore Kennel Club
Mr. N. Udaychander(Hon.Sec)
699, Avinashi Road,
Coimbatore -641037
Ph: 91-(0)422-211266

Canine Club of Kolhapur
Dr. L.P.Kapdi (Hon. Sec)
5, Sai Prasad Korgaongar
Housing Society,
13, Lane, Rajarampuri,
Kolhapur - 416008

Silchar Kennel Club
Mr. B.B. Mahapatra (Hon. Sec)
Dass Brothers Building
Central Road, **Silchar** - 788001
Off Ph: 91-(0)3842-34606
Res Ph: 91-(0)3842-32573

Table 2 : Addresses of KCI members authorized for judging

Place	Name	Address
Amritsar	Mr.Yogesh Tuteja	71, Dayanand Nagar, III, Lawrence Road, Amritsar. Phone:- 222612
Bangalore	Mr.Shantha Ram	96, Rathnavilasa Road, Basavanagudi Bangalore – 560 004

Bangalore	Mr.Thukaram	297, 26th Cross, Banashankari II Stage Bangalore – 560 070
Mumbai	Ms.Sheila Naharwar	9, Garden Homes 1st Road, Khar(W) Bombay – 400 052 Phone: - 022-24030642/24405159
Delhi	Mr.Rajiv Shandilya	3500, Kuchalalman Darya Gung New Delhi – 110 002 Phone: - 011-23241028
Delhi	Mr.Mukul Vaid	House No.36, Lane W-22 Western Avenue, Sainik Farm New Delhi – 110 062 Phone: 09810402598 0911129552804
Calicut	Mr.Santhosh	Thampisons Electronics Mavoor Road, Calicut – 673 004 Phone: - 0495-2744640 Mob: - 09846444640
Chandigarh	Maj.Trilochan Singh	Maj.Trilochan Singh 1156, Sector – 33 C Chandigarh
Coimbatore	Mr.P.Balasubramaniam	156, Tea Estates Race Course, Coimbatore 641 018 Phone: - 0422-2221311
Jalandhar	Mr.Jagteswar Singh	Tarlochan Villa 4, New Friends Colony, Near Radha Swami Satsang Bhavan Nabha Dist. Patiala Punjab Phone: - 01765-221634
Orissa	Mr.S.R. Prusti	Nalini 3/A, Budheswari Area Bhubaneswar – 751 006 Phone: 3129101/312115
Lucknow	Mr.K.K. Trivedi	C-784, Sector –C, Mahanagar, Lucknow – 226 006 (UP) Phone: - 0522-2331174/0415020510

Kanpur	Mr.P.S. Munjal	Architect, 118/442-E, Kaushalpuri, Kanpur - 12 (UP)
Pune	Mr.Sanjay Desai	"Desai House" 177/2, Dhole Patil Road Pune 411 001 Phone:-020-26004100, 26004155
Silchar	Mr.Mahapatra	Dass Brothers' Buildings Central Road, Silchar - 788 001 Phone: - (03842)22606
Ooty	Ms.Sunitha Srinivasan	Sans Souci Noonsouci PO 643 238 Nilgiris
Agra	Mr.S.P.Malik	Malikville 9, Tagore Nagar, Heera Bagh Agra - 282 005 Phone: - 91-562-2570789
Trivandrum	Dr.Sukumaran Nair	Sreenilayam VP 11/240, Ranni Lane Perrorkada P.O Thiruvananthapuram -695 005 Phone: - 0471-2374779
Dehradun	Mr.Dev Lahiri	Welham Boy's School Dehradun - 248 001
Kolkata	Mr.Sib Sankar Chatterjee	46, Durgapur Lane Plot No.302, 3rd Floor Kolkata 700 027. Phone: 033-24030642(o)24405158 (R)

❑❑❑

Chapter 27
Insurance

Dogs, like other precious commodities, can be insured against death due to accident and/or diseases. Many insurance companies have launched dog insurance scheme. Some of them are as follows:

1. The Oriental Insurance Company Limited
   A-25/27 Asaf Ali Road, New Delhi-110002
   Website: http://www.orientalinsurance.org.in/portal/dt
2. The New India Assurance Company Limited
   87, M.G. Road, Fort, Mumbai-400001
   Website: http://www.newindia.co.in/index1.asp
3. The National Insurance Company Limited
   3-Middleton Streets, Kolkata-700071
   Website: www.nationalinsuranceindia.com
4. The United India Insurance Company Limited
   24, Whites Road, Chennai-600014
   Website: http://www.uiic.co.in/

Scope of cover, terms and conditions, premium rate and claim procedure slightly differs from one company to other, though their basic features are almost identical. Common features of different insurance schemes are as follows:

1. Indigenous, cross bred or exotic breeds, which are pets, watch dogs, sheep dogs and hunting dogs, all can be insured.
2. Dogs only in the age group of 8 weeks to 8 years can be insured.
3. Valuation of the dog is to be done by any (or company's specified) veterinary doctor at the time of insurance, who will issue a certificate for this purpose.

Documents required at the time of insurance:

1. Duly filled application form.
2. Veterinary health certificate in prescribed format. It should clearly mention breed, sex, age and identification mark of the dog.
3. Vaccination record
4. Kennel club registration certificate, if available.
5. Identification of dog: Any one of 3 methods including tattooing, nose print or photograph is acceptable. Now a days, electronic identification system is also available.

Coverage: Death due to accident/or diseases contracted during the period of insurance.

Extended coverage: For extended coverages, company charges extra premium. It includes:

1. Death by accident in transit by air, rail, road and water and show risks.
2. Death by accidental poisoning.
3. Breeding risks, like death during whelping, death of newborn pups etc. Sum insured against the loss of pups should not exceed the sum insured for bitch.
4. Lost or stolen dogs.
5. Loss of show entry fee, when dog is unable to attend dog show because of accident or disease covered by the policy.
6. Liability for personal injuries and damage to property (including animals, poultry) of third parties.
7. Risk during travel abroad.

Exclusions

1. Death due to malicious poisoning, intentional killing or death due to owner negligence.
2. Partial or permanent disability of any nature.
3. Death due to diseases like Distemper, Rabies, Viral Hepatitis, Leptospirosis, Viral enteritis. These diseases are covered only if the dog has been properly vaccinated against these diseases at the time of insurance.
4. Death occurring prior to and within 15 days of insurance.

Claim procedure

1. Intimate the insuring company immediately after death of the dog.
2. Submit following documents:
    1. Duly completed claim form.
    2. Veterinary certificate for death on Company's form giving market value of the dog at the time of death and cause of death.
    3. Postmortem report.
    4. Photograph of the dog taken just after the death.

Indemnity

Company usually bears only 80% of the market value of the dog at the time of death or sum insured, whichever is less. Rest 20% of the claim amount is to be borne by the insured. Market value of the dog is to be certified by the Veterinary Doctor.

❑❑❑

Chapter 28

Internet Resources

There is plethora of information available on internet. The need is to find a suitable site that can provide authentic information. Remember, the information given on all the sites are not necessarily accurate, correct, complete or reliable. Check for site ownership, authorship of contents, audience and perspective of the site. Many information may be misleading. Online purchase is never without a risk. So avoid them, as far as possible. Some internet resources related to dog are given below.

1. Kennel Clubs

   a. Kennel Club of India, Chennai: http://www.thekci.org/

   b. The Kennel Club (UK): http://www.thekennelclub.org.uk

   c. American Kennel Club: http://www.akc.org/

   Important informations related to registration of dog, dog shows etc. are available on the website of Kennel Club of India. The Kennel Club (UK) and American Kennel Club websites also provide detailed information related to dog breeds, health aspects, vaccination etc.

2. Sale and Purchase of pups, dog accessories, pet foods etc.
   a. www.olx.in
   b. http://www.entirelypets.com/
   c. www.justdial.com
   d. http://www.vetvax.com/
   e. http://www.drsfostersmith.com/Default.cfm
3. Diseases and health care
   a. http://www.petmd.com/
   b. http://www.dogchatforum.com/
   c. www.healthypet.com/: The American Animal Hospital Association website that provides information related to dog behaviour, dog care, matters related to traveling with pets and link to veterinarians.
   d. www.peteducation.com: For articles related to allergies, anatomy, normal values of different parameters, behaviour and training, cancer and tumors, dental care and oral diseases, digestive system, ears, eyes, first aid and emergency care, fleas and ticks, grooming and sanitation, heart and respiratory system, hormones, housing, play, travel, human animal bond, immune and blood system, infections, liver and pancreas, nerve and muscle condition, puppy care, nutrition and feeding, parasites and worms, reproduction, senior dog care, skin conditions, spaying and neutering, urinary system, vaccines and vaccinations, veterinary examinations etc.
   e. http://www.dogchatforum.com/: Deals with behavioral problems, common health problems, articles related to training, breeding and other managemental aspects.
4. Books/ Dictionaries/ Reading materials
   a. The Merck Veterinary Manual: www.merckvetmanual.com/mvm/index.jsp
   b. Veterinary dictionary:
      http://www.peteducation.com/dict_alpha_listing.cfm?c=0
      http://www.vetmed.wsu.edu/glossary/glossary.asp
   c. Vet Abbreviations & Acronyms:
      www.library.uiuc.edu/vex/vetdocs/abbreviation.htm

5. *Search engines*: They are also called as information gateways. Type a keyword (important word) related to the information you want, the site will search give a list of related links. Good search engines are listed below.
   a. GOOGLE: http://www.google.co.in/
   b. YAHOO: http://www.yahoo.com/
   c. ALTA VISTA: http://www.altavista.com/
   d. WIKIPEDIA: http://en.wikipedia.org/wiki/Main_Page
   e. AOL SEARCH: http://search.aol.com/aol/webhome
   f. GIGABLAST: http://www.gigablast.com/
   g. MSN SEARCH: http://www.msn.com/
   h. JOEANT: http://www.joeant.com/
   i. LYCOS: http://www.lycos.com/
   j. MAMMA: http://www.mamma.com/
   k. DMOZ OPEN DIRECTORY: http://www.dmoz.org/
   l. WEBCRAWLER: http://www.webcrawler.com/
   m. ALL THE WEB: http://www.alltheweb.com/
6. International organizations dealing with pet and human health
   a. O.I.E.: www.oie.int
   b. F.A.O.: www.fao.org/ag/againfo/subjects/en/health/default.html
   c. W.H.O.: http://www.who.int/en/
7. Import, travel, training, breeds, nutrition etc.
   a. http://www.ieport.com Import of dogs
   b. http://clickertraining.com/: Training
   c. www.pettravel.com: Travel with pet
   d. www.puppypurebred.com: Dog breed information
   e. www.vetinfo4dogs.com: Veterinary information for dog owners
   f. www.petfoodreport.com: Pet foods
   g. http://www.indiakennels.com/index.php

8. *Sites of local service providers*:
   a. www.petvacation.in: Bombay based website, that deals with various aspects of dog care and management, transportation, importation etc. and offer paid shelter for dogs and cats when you are going out of station for a long time.
   b. www.shevar.com: Bangalore based site that provides hydrotherapy, ice-cream bath, detangling, hair cutting and clipping, basic hygiene, anti-tick and flea treatment, scaling of teeth, massage, bath and grooming.
   c. http://www.dogsindia.com/: Chennai based sites providing information and services related to puppies, breeders, doggy products, vets and training
9. Videos/ slide show related to dog care, treatment etc.
   a. Veterinary videos: http://vetvideos.com/
   b. Google video: http://www.youtube.com
   c. U Tube: http://www.youtube.com/
   d. E how: http://www.ehow.com/
   e. Slide download: http://www.slideshare.net
10. Animal welfare related sites:
   a. People for Ethical Treatment of Animals (PETA, Headquarter-Mumbai): http://www. petaindia.com/
   b. Beauty Without Cruelty (BWC, Headquarter- Poona): http://www.bwcindia.org/weborms/Default.aspx
   c. People for Animals (PFA): http://www.peopleforanimals.org
   d. Ministry of Environment and Forests, Government of India: http://moef.nic.in/modules/rules-and-regulations/animal-welfare
   e. Animal Welfare Board of India: http://www.awbi.org/
   f. List and address of animal welfare organizations working in India:

      i. http://www.weforanimals.com/animals%20welfare%20organizations/animals%20welfare%20organizations.html

      ii. http://www.charitiesindia.org.2008/06/animal-welfare-organizations-in-india.html

      iii. http://www.avma.org/: Official website of American Veterinary Medical Association

❑❑❑

Chapter 29 Appendices

Appendix 1 : Abbreviations used in prescription writing

Abbreviation	Meaning	Abbreviation	Meaning
a.c.	Before giving food	stat.	Immediately
ad lib	Freely as wanted	Sus.	Suspension
aq	Water	Syr.	Syrup
b.i.d.	Twice daily	Tab.	Tablet
b.wt.	Body weight	t.i.d.	Three times a day
$\bar{c}$	With	p.o.	Orally/ by mouth
cap	Capsule	I/M	Intramuscular
o.d.	Once daily	I/V	Intravenous
p.c.	After giving food	I/P	Intraperitoneal
p.r.n.	As occasion requires	$\bar{s}$	without
q2h	Every two hourly	S/C	Subcutaneously
s.i.d.	Once daily	t.s.f.	Tea spoon ful (5 ml)
Sol.	Solution	I/U	Intrauterine
s.o.s.	If necessary		

Appendix 2 : Normal biological parameters

Parameter	Average value
Life span	12 years
Rectal temperature	101.5±1.5(^{0}F)
Respiration rate	20-40 breaths/ minute
Heart rate	70-180 beats/ minute
Water requirement	25-35 ml/kg body weight/day
Metabolic energy requirement	65 K Cal/ kg body weight/ day

Note: Values for a given parameter varies with breed. Above values are more proximate for those breeds in which body weight of an adult varies from 15 to 35 kg.

Appendix 3 : Normal reproductive parameters

Parameter	Average value
Breeding season	Twice a year, once in August- September; second in March April. But it may continue round the year
Gestation period	59-68 days
Estrus duration	9-10 days
Sexual maturity (male and female)	6-12 months
Best time for mating	In between 9 to 14 days after first bleeding. Allow to mate on alternate days for three times
Breeding life (male and female)	6-8 years
Litter size	1 to 12 (depends upon the breed)

Appendix 4 : Growth physiology and developmental stages in pups

Function	Age
Opening of eyes	10-12 days
Start bearing weight on legs	7-10 days
Optimum time for weaning (separating from mother)	6-8 weeks
Temporary tooth eruption	3-4 weeks
Permanent tooth eruption	4-6 months

Appendix 5 : Normal haematogical parameters of dog

Haematological parameters	
Parameter	**Normal range**
Total blood volume/ kg body weight	80-90 ml
Haemoglobin (g/ dL)	14.2-19.2
Packed Cell Volume (%)	29-55
Red Blood Cell count (x 10^6/ µL)	5.5-8.5
MCHC (g/ dL)	32-36
MCV (fL)	60-80
MCH (pg)	22-27
Thrombocytes (x 10^6/ µL)	200-900
White Blood Cell count (x 10^6/ µL)	6.0-17.1
Neutrophils (mature) (x 10^6/ µL)	3.6-11.5
Lymphocytes (x 10^6/ µL)	1.0-4.8
Monocytes (x 10^6/ µL)	0.15-1.35
Eosinophils (x 10^6/ µL)	0.01-1.25
Basophil (/ µL)	0-1

Appendix 6 : Normal blood biochemical parameters

Parameter	**Normal range**
Sodium (mEq/L)	140-151
Potassium (mEq/L)	3.4-5.4
Chloride (mEq/L)	105-120
Bicarbonate (mEq/L)	15-25
Anion gap (mEq/L)	13-25
Calcium (mg/ dL)	9.5-12
Phosphorus (mg/ dL)	3.3-6.8
Magnesium (mg/ dL)	1.5-2.7
Iron (mg/ dL)	84-233
Bi-carbonate (m Eq/ L)	17-24
Cholesterol (mg/ dL)	110-314
Triglycerides (mg/ dL)	58-65
Glucose (mg/ dL)	65-130
A/G ratio	0.53-3.5

contd...

Total protein (g/ dL)	5.2-7.2
Albumin (g/dL)	2.5-4.3
Creatinine (mg/ dL)	0.4-1.4
Total bilirubin (mg/ dL)	0.2-0.8
Conjugated bilirubin (mg/ dL)	0-0.30
Uric acid (mg/ dL)	0-2.0
Amylase (U/L)	286-1124
Lipase (U/L)	120-258
ALT(IU/L)	10-120
ALP(IU/ L)	20-150
AST(IU/L)	15-40
GGT(IU/L)	1-5
Amylase (IU/L)	200-1290
Creatinine kinase (IU/L)	20-200
LDH (IU/L)	30-190
Urea nitrogen (mg/ dL)	6-24
T_3 (ng/ dL)	48-154
T_4 (ng/ dL)	1.0-4.7

Appendix 7 : Normal urine analysis values

Parameter	Normal value
Volume (mL/kg/day)	24-40
Specific gravity	1.015-1.045
pH	6.0-7.0
Colour	Yellow-amber
Odour	Ammonical
Appearance	Clear
Protein	Negative- Trace
Glucose	Negative
Ketones	Negative
Urobilinogen	Negative
Bilirubin	Negative
Cells	0-8 RBC or WBC per high power field
Casts	0-2 hyaline or granular cast per high power field

Appendix 8 : Normal blood coagulation profile

Parameter	Normal value
Bleeding time (minutes)	1-5
Clotting time of whole blood (minutes)	3-13
Activated Clotting Time (minutes)	1-2
Partial thromboplastic Time (APTT, seconds)	11-19
Prothrombin Time (OSPT/PT, seconds)	5-12
Thrombin Time (TCT, seconds)	3-8
Fibrin Degradation Products (FDP, µg/mL)	< 32

Appendix 9 : Diseases common in different dog breeds

Breed	Disorders
Cocker Spanial	Skin problems, kidney failure, eye diseases (glaucoma, cataract, retinal atrophy), epilepsy (fits), obesity
Blood Hound	Eye diseases
Boxer	Heart diseases (cardiomyopathy), blindness, bone and joint problems (arthritis), skin problem, mouth and gum tumors, epilepsy
Bull Terrier	Deafness, dystocia, kidney failure, heart and skin diseases
Chihuahua	Eye problems (glaucoma), epilepsy
Chow Chow	Bone and joint diseases, eye problems, behavioural problems (aggressiveness)
Dachshunds	Bone and joint disease, eye problem (retinal atrophy), kidney failure, epilepsy
Dalmatian	Deafness, urinary problems (kidney failure, stones)
Doberman Pinscher	Deafness, heart diseases, kidney failure, joint diseases
German Shepherd	Joint (hip/elbow) dislocation, cataract, gastric problems, epilepsy, blindness
Golden Retriever	Hip dysplasia, eye diseases (retinal atrophy, cataract, entropion), epilepsy
Great Dane	Bone and joint diseases, deafness, hear diseases
Labrador Retriever	Obesity, bone and joint diseases, eye diseases (retinal atrophy, cataract, blindness, entropion), epilepsy
Mastiff	Hip dysplasia, eye lid problems (entropion), stomach problems

contd...

Pekingese	Bone and joint diseases, eye problems, respiratory problems, heat stroke
Rottweiler	Deafness, bone and joint diseases
Shar Pei	Skin diseases, eye diseases, kidney diseases
St. Bernard	Joint (hip/elbow) dislocation, eye-lid problems, hair fall
Poodle	Eye problems (progressive retinal atrophy), retained milk teeth
Old English Sheepdog	Hip dysplasia, cataract, heart problems (cardiomyopathy)
Bull dog	Infertility, poor nursing, eye problems, skin problems, allergy, respiratory problems
Mastiff	Poor nursing ability
Collie	Blindness
Beagle	Epilepsy
Spitz	Stomach Problems
Pug	Eye diseases, obesity, joint, bone, heart and respiratory problems

Deworming and Vaccination Record

Name of Dog	**Breed**
Age	**Sex**
Identification mark	**Registration no.**

Owner's Name and Address

Photograph of the dog

Deworming

Date	Name of Dewormer	Next due date	Signature of veterinarian

Vaccination

Date	Name of Vaccine and Batch Number	Next due date	Signature of veterinarian

❑❑❑

Chapter 30

Common Names of Dog

A

Ace
Action
Admiral
Affinity
Ajay
Akira
Aladdin
Ali Baba
Alpha
Alpine
Amazon
Ambassador
Amber
Ammo
Anaconda
Angel
Apollo
Aquarius
Archie
Argus
Ariel
Aries
Aristotle
Armani
Arty
Ashes
Astro
Atlas
Auditor
Austin
Avanti

B

Baba
Babe
Babs
Babushka
Baby
Baby-Doll
Baby-Face
Bacon
Baja
Bali
Bambi
Bambino
Bangle
Banjo
Barbarian
Barbarino
Baron
Bazooka
Beans
Bear
Beauty

Belladonna
Belle
Bessie
Big Boy
Bimbo
Bina
Bingo
Birdy
Bishop
Bismarck
Blackie
Blossom
Blueberry
Bob
Bobo
Bolero
Bongo
Bono
Bonsai
Bookie
Boom-Boom
Boris
Boss
Bossman
Bouncer
Boxer
Brandy
Brassy
Bravo
Breathless
Brew
Brit
Broadway
Brown Sugar
Brownie
Bruno
Bubba
Bubbles
Buck
Buckingham
Bud
Buddy
Buffy
Bug
Bullet
Bullion
Bum
Bumper
Bumpkin
Bunk
Bunny
Burger
Burma
Buster
Butch
Butter
Buzz
Buzzard
Byron
Byte

C

Cabo
Cadbury
Caddy
Cadet
Caesar
Cairo
Cajun
Calamity
Caliber
California
Calvin
Came
Camelot
Candy
Canis
Capricorn
Captain
Carg
Carnation
Carraway
Casanova
Casey
Cash
Cashmere
Casino
Casper
Caspian
Cassie
Catalina
Catamaran
Caviar
Cecil
Cha-Cha
Challenger
Champion
Chanel
Chaos
Chaplin
Charmer
Chaya
Check
Cheetah
Chelsea
Chester
Chewy
Cheyenne
Chic
Chico
Chief
Chili
China
Chin-Chin
Chip
Chipper
Chips
Cho Mein
Chocolate

Cholo
Choo-Choo
Chopin
Chopper
Chopsticks
Chubby
Chump
Chunk
Chunky
Churchill
Chutney
Ciao
Cinnamon
Cinnamon
Circe
Cisco
Citron
Citrus
Classy
Clipper
Clone
Clover
Coconut
Cody
Cola
Colonel
Colt
Comet
Condor
Confection
Conga
Congo
Cookie
Copper
Coral
Cordial
Cori
Corona
Coronet
Cory
Cosmo
Cracker Crash Cricket
Crier
Crimson
Cristyl
Cruiser
Crumb
Crumpet
Crusader
Crystal
Cubby Cucina
Cuckoo
Cuddles
Curious George
Curly
Curry
Cutie Cypress
Cyrano

D

Daisy
Dal
Damage
Dancer
Dank
Daredevil
Dash
Dasher
Dawn
Dazzler
Delilah
Delta
Detonator
Detour
Devil
Dew
Diamond
Dice
Dingo
Dino
Diva
Divot
Dixie
Dizzy
Doc
Dodo
Dolly
Domino
Don
Doogie
Dots
Dozer
Draco
Dragon
Dreamer
Droopy
Drummer Dude
Duffy
Duke
Dumpling
Dun
Duncan
Dunk
Dusty Dynamite
Dynamo

E

Echo
Eclipse Edge
Eggo
Einstein Elias
Elmer Elvira
Elvis
Emerson
Emily
Emma
Epic
Epstein

Equity
Escort
Eskimo

F

Face
Fancy
Fang
Fantasia
Fats
Fatso
Fatty
Fedora
Felix
Fennel
Fido
Fifi
Fiji
Firebug
Fizz
Flapper
Flash
Fletch
Flipper
Flirt
Flora or Fauna
Flower
Fluffy
Flurry
Football
Foxy
Freebie
Friday
Frisky
Frosty
Fuchsia
Funky
Furball
Furface
Furr
Fuzzie

G

Galileo
Gambler
Garbo
Garlic
Gatekeeper
Gator
Geezer
Geisha
Gemini
Genie
Genius
Georgia
Giddy
Gideon
Giggles
Gigi
Gigolo
Gin
Ginger
Gipper
Gobble
Goblin
Godzilla
Goldie
Gorgeous
Gorilla
Gorky Grace Grazie
Gremlin
Grizzly
Grover
Grumpy
Grunt
Gumball
Gumbo
Gumby
Gunner
Guru
Gusto
Guy
Gypsy
Gyro

H

Ham
Hamlet
Hammer
Handsome
Hansel
Happy
Hard Rock
Hardy Harmony
Harvey
Havana
Hawk
Hawkeye
Hazer
Hearts
Heaven
Hedgehog
Hefty
Heidi
Heiress Herman
Hero
Hippo
Historia Hocus-Pocus
Hog
Holly
Homer
Homey
Honey
Honeybee Rose
Hood
Hoofman
Hook

Hoover
Hope
Horace
Horus
Hot Dog
Hotshot Howard
Howler
Hubble
Hudson
Hulk
Humphrey
Hunter
Hyde

I

Iceman Icon
Iggy
Ignatius
Indiana
Indie
Indigo
Infinity
Inky
Intelectus
Iodine
Iris
Irresistible
Ishta

J

Jackpot
Jade
Jag
Jamaica
Jasmine
Jasper
Java
Jazz
Jed
Jedi
Jelly-Belly
Jemima
Jerky
Jersey
Jet
Jingles
Jinx
Joker
Joy
Jubilee
Judge
Juliet
Jumbo
June
Junior
Juniper
Jupiter

K

Kahlua
Karma
Kid
Kiki
Kiku
Killer
King
Kiwi
Knockout
Koko
Kool
Kosmic
Kosmo
Krispy
Kuma

L

Lacey
Laser
Lassie
Lavender
Leila
Lemon
Leo
Levi
Liberty
Lilac
Link
Lion
Lira
Lobo
Lola
Lolita
Lolly
Loony
Lotus
Lovey
Lucky
Lulu
Lunatic

M

Mac
Macho Maestro
Maggie
Magna
Magnet
Mamba
Mambo
Mamie
Manchu
Mandy
Marble
Marigold
Martini
Matador
Matilda
Mattie

Matzo
Max
Maya Medusa Mellow
Melody
Mercedes
Metro
Miata
Mickey
Midnight
Miles
Mink
Minnie
Mogul
Mohave
Mohawk
Mole
Mona
Mona Lisa
Monk
Monty
Moody
Moonmist
Moonshine
Moose
Mopsy
Mouton
Moxie
Mozart
Muffin
Mulberry
Muse
Mutant
Mystic
Myth

N

Napoleon
Nappy
Neon
Newton
Nibbles
Nikita
Niko
Nina
Nitro
Novella
Nugget
Nutmeg
Nymph

P

Pagoda
Pal
Panama
Panda
Pandora
Pansy
Panther
Papu
Paradise
Paragon
Paris
Patsy
Penne
Pepe
Pepper
Perro
Peso
Petra
Piazza
Picasso
Ping
Pinky
Piper
Pippi
Pistol
Piston
Pluto
Poco
Poet
Pogo
Polo
Pong
Pongo
Precious
President
Pretty
Pretty Baby
Prima Donna
Primo
Prince or Princess
Puck
Pudding
Puff
Puffball
Puppy
Pygmy

Q

Qantas
Queeny
Quiche
Quick

R

Radar
Ragu
Raider
Rain
Rainbow
Rajah
Rambo
Ranger
Ravel
Raven
Ray
Razz

Reebok
Remy
Reno
Repo
Rex
Rhea
Rhino
Rhodes
Ricotta
Rider
Ringleader
Ringo
Rio
Ripley
Ripple
Rock
Rocker
Rocket
Rocky
Rococo
Roma
Romeo
Rooster
Rosarita
Rosebud
Rosie
Rover
Rowdy
Royal
Ruby
Runner
Runt
Rusty

S

Sadie
Safari
Saffron
Saga
Sahara
Sailor
Salsa
Salty
Sam
Sammy
Samson
Santo
Sasha
Sashimi
Scarlet
Schooner
Scintilla
Scoobie
Scorpio
Scotch
Scuba
Seal
Seneca
Sera
Seychelles
Shadow
Shah
Shalimar
Shamu
Sharp
Sheba
Sheer
Sheik
Sheriff
Sherlock
Shiksa
Shim Shim
Shiva
Shooter
Shotgun
Shrimp
Shylock
Sidney
Sierra
Silky
Silver
Sin
Singer
Sky
Sky Hawk
Skywalker
Slate
Slicker
Sloth
Smasher
Smokey
Smoocher
Snaker
Snap
Sneezy
Sniffer
Snooker
Snooper
Snoopy
Snooty
Snow, Snowball
Snowberry
Snowman
Snuffle
Socks
Solo
Solomon
Sonata
Sooner
Sophie
Sorbet
Spades
Spago
Spam
Spanky
Sparkle
Sparrow
Speedy
Sphinx

Spicy
Spider
Spike
Spinner
Spirit
Splash
Sport
Spot
Sprite
Sputnik
Spy
Star
Stargazer
Starlet
Stella
Stellar
Sting
Stinky
Stoli
Stoney
Storm or Stormy
Stubby
Stump
Sugar
Sulfur
Sultan
Sumo
Suni
Sunkiss
Sunrise
Sunshine
Sushi
Swami
Swampy Sweetie
Swizzle
Synergy

T

Taffy
Tag
Tampest
Tang
Tango
Tanner
Tara
Taro
Tarot
Tarzan
Tattoo
Taurus
Taz
Teaser
Terminator
Terror
Texas
Thai
Thistle
Thunder
Tiara
Tiger
Tiny
Tipsy
Titan
Toad
Toby
Tofu
Topaz
Tornado
Toro
Toto
Touché
Tova
Tramp
Treat
Trojan
Troll
Tropicana
Trump
Tryst
Tuffy
Tulip
Tuna
Turbo
Tutti-Frutti
Tutu
Tweety
Twinkle
Twister
Tycoon
Typhoon

U

Uma
Umpa
Uranus
Urchin
Ursa
Utopia

V

Vagabond
Valentine
Valentino
Vanilla
Veggie
Velvet
Venus
Violet
Viper
Visa
Viva
Voodoo

W

Wags
Waldo
Wanda

Warrior
Web
Whiskey
Whisper or Wilson
Wimpy
Windy
Wink
Winston
Wizard
Woody
Wooly Wrangler

X

Xavier
Xena

Y

Yahoo
Yoda
Yogi Bear
You Too
Yo-Yo
Yummy

Z

Zack
Zaire
Zepellin
Zero
Zeus
Zodiac
Zoe
Zsa Zsa
Zuni

❑❑❑

Colour Plates

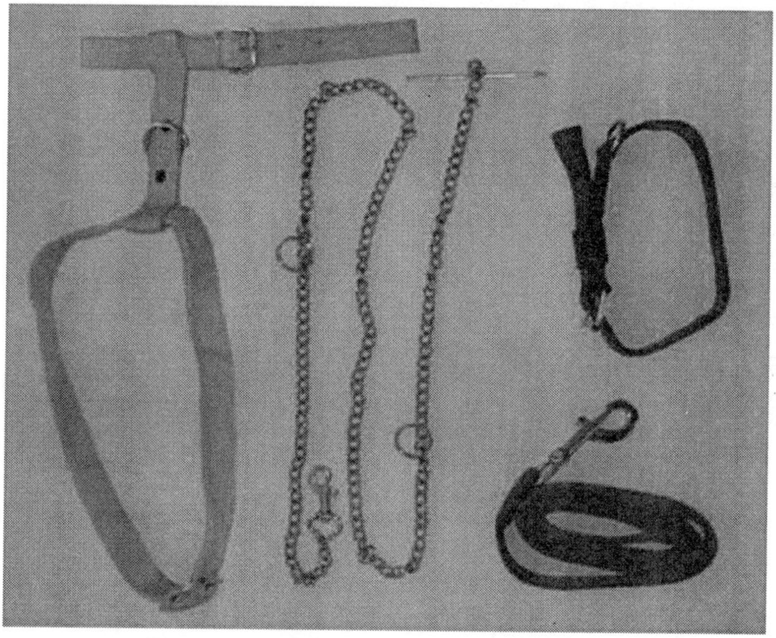

Fig. 1 : Different types of collar and lead

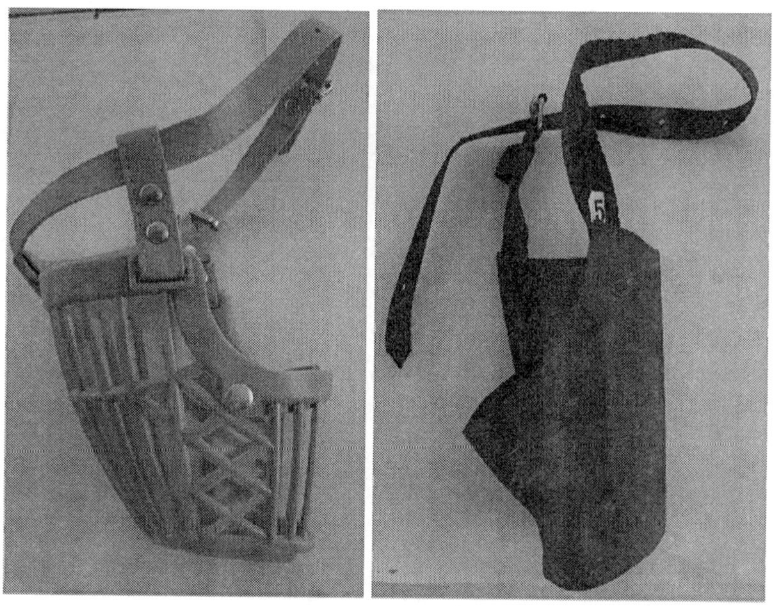

Fig. 2 : Two different types of dog muzzle

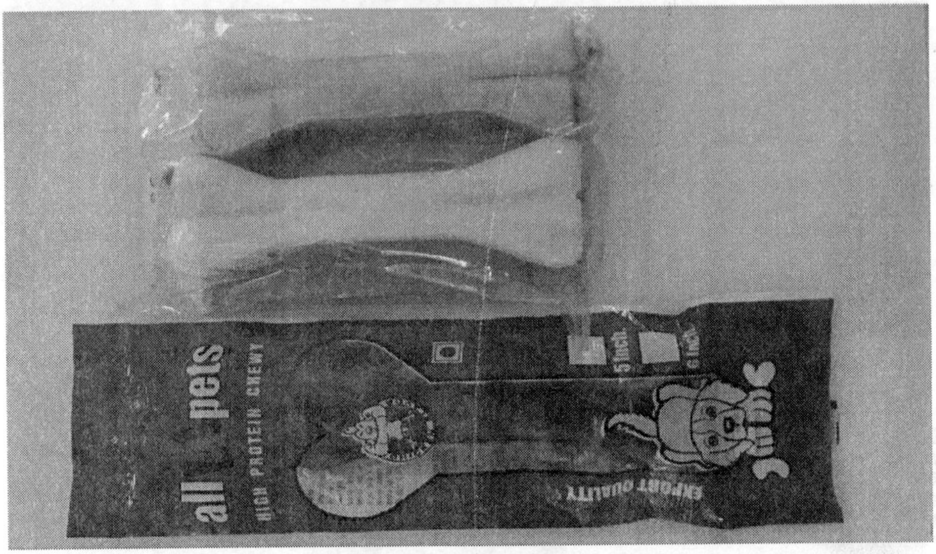

Fig. 3 : Dog chews

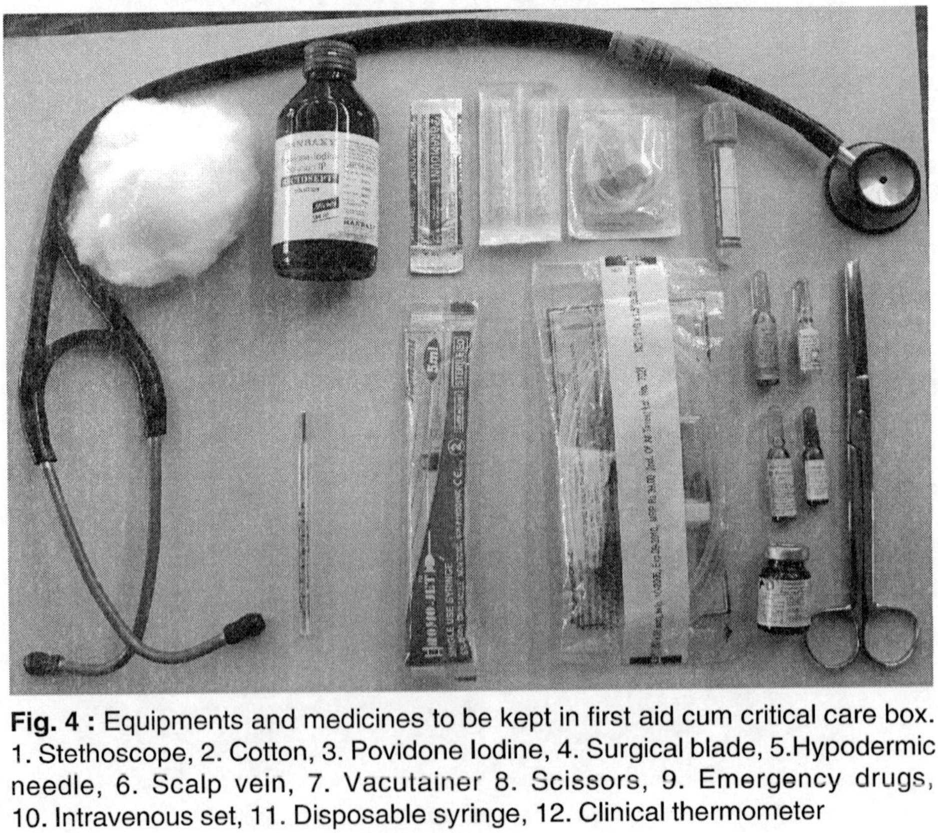

Fig. 4 : Equipments and medicines to be kept in first aid cum critical care box. 1. Stethoscope, 2. Cotton, 3. Povidone Iodine, 4. Surgical blade, 5.Hypodermic needle, 6. Scalp vein, 7. Vacutainer 8. Scissors, 9. Emergency drugs, 10. Intravenous set, 11. Disposable syringe, 12. Clinical thermometer

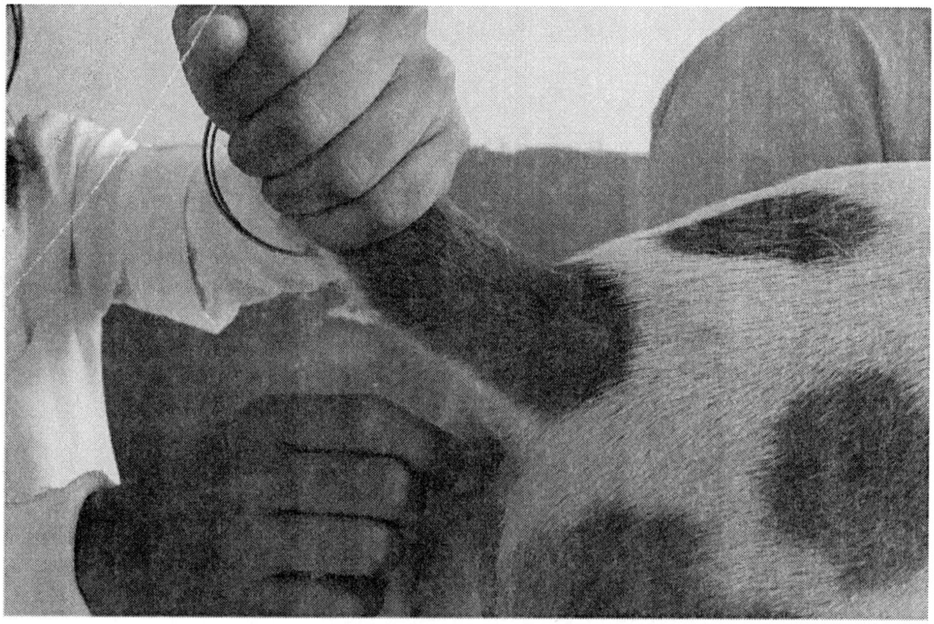

Fig. 5 : Recording of rectal temperature

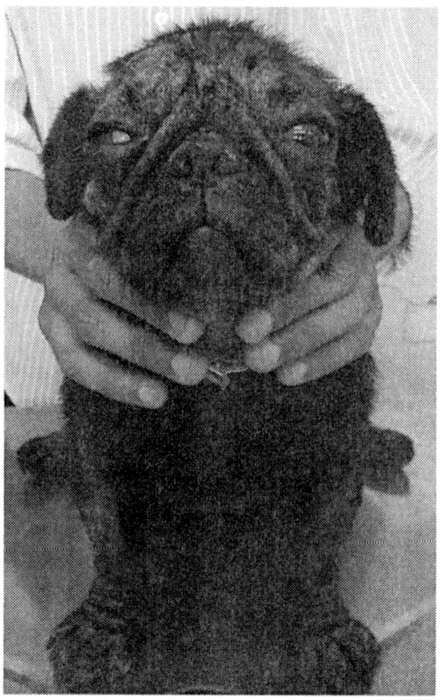

Fig. 6 : Skin problems are common in dogs

About the Author

Amita Ranjan : Did her graduation in Veterinary Science and Animal Husbandry in 2006 and Masters (Veterinary Pharmacology and Toxicology) in 2008 from Ranchi Veterinary College, Birsa Agricultural University, Jharkhand. She received Radha Harihar Prasad Memorial gold medal during B.V.Sc. & A.H. She is having a brilliant academic record throughout her carrier. In year 1997, received Award of Honour from Chief Minister, Bihar for securing second position in the matriculation examination. She was selected in "National Talent Search Examination" in 1996-97 and got distinction in Biology and Physics in the Intermediate examination in year 1999. Presently, she is doing Ph.D. from Guru Angad Dev Veterinary and Animal Sciences University, Ludhiana, Punjab and receiving Senior Research Fellowship (SRF) from ICAR, New Delhi. She has also qualified ICAR-NET in year 2010. She has published several research papers in different International and National Journals of repute. She is a pet lover and has good expertise in care, management and treatment of dogs. She enjoys providing clinical services to sick dogs during leisure time.